JOHN DRYDEN'S
Imagery

JOHN DRYDEN'S
Imagery

by

ARTHUR W. HOFFMAN

University of Florida Press
Gainesville

TO MY MOTHER

AND

TO THE MEMORY OF MY FATHER

A University of Florida Press Book

PUBLISHED WITH ASSISTANCE
FROM
THE FORD FOUNDATION

LIBRARY OF CONGRESS CARD CATALOGUE NUMBER: 61-14910
LITHOPRINTED BY ROSE PRINTING COMPANY
TALLAHASSEE, FLORIDA

Preface

HIS STUDY OF Dryden is indebted in a large way to Dryden himself because he talked—and some writers do not—about what he was doing and what other writers had done, because he contended for subjects and methods, and because he willingly displayed some of the changes of his mind and art. Samuel Johnson heads a succession of instigative critics without whom the discussion of Dryden could not be what it now is. Assertions by T. S. Eliot, Mark Van Doren, Louis Bredvold, Ruth Wallerstein, E. M. W. Tillyard, and Samuel Holt Monk, beyond those recorded in the text and notes, have jogged my hand and, I hope, my mind. I am indebted, of course, to Dryden's editors, H. T. Swedenberg, Jr., and the late Edward Niles Hooker, to James Kinsley, and particularly to the late George R. Noyes to whom all consideration of Dryden is in debt.

Syracuse University, in the spring of 1959, granted me a leave of absence which helped substantially to bring this study toward final form and publication.

Lewis F. Haines, Director, his wife Helen, Production Manager, and Paul Chalker, Assistant Editor, of the University of Florida Press, have been helpful and kind.

Reference librarians at Yale and at Syracuse have assisted patiently.

Maynard Mack directed this study in its original form as a Yale dissertation; he shed light on every problem that arose.

I am indebted also to the generous assistance, lively conversation, and patient listening of my friends, Aubrey Williams and David R. Clark.

And my wife, Joyce, and daughters, Ruth and Gail, have been the Miranda of the voyage.

ARTHUR W. HOFFMAN

Syracuse, New York
January, 1962

A NOTE ON THE TEXT OF DRYDEN

Dryden's poems, in this study, are cited from the California edition of Dryden's works (*The Works of John Dryden,* general editors Edward Niles Hooker and H. T. Swedenberg, Jr., University of California Press, Berkeley and Los Angeles, 1956, Volume I: *Poems 1649-1680*) and the edition of Dryden's poetry by James Kinsley (*The Poems of John Dryden,* ed. James Kinsley, Oxford University Press, Oxford, 1958, 4 volumes). Volume I of the California edition, the only volume that has so far appeared, contains poetry published between 1649 and 1680, but with the omission of the prologues and epilogues of Dryden's own plays. Page references to both editions are given for poems that appear in both, though the text reproduced is then that of the California edition. The same practice is followed for prose dedications, prefaces, and prefatory essays printed in these editions.

References to these editions are given in abbreviated form directly following quotations of poetry, volume number, page numbers, followed by the symbol "C" for the California edition and "K" for Professor Kinsley's edition. The same form of abbreviation is used to locate prose passages.

Table of Contents

Preface, v

Introduction, ix

1. *An Apprenticeship in Praise, 1*

2. *Prologues and Epilogues, 20*

3. *A Layman's Faith, 55*

4. *Absalom and Achitophel, 72*

5. *To Mr. Oldham and To Anne Killigrew, 92*

6. *Various John Dryden, 130*

Epilogue, 148

Index, 169

Introduction

HE SUBJECT OF Dryden's imagery and of his poetic style in general has excited, in the two and a half centuries since his death, a surprising diversity of critical comment. Samuel Johnson, for example, both belabored him for extravagance and praised him for propriety. Sir Walter Scott bemoaned his conceits, while Matthew Arnold accused his poetry of all the virtues of good prose. It is apparent that the variety of these well-known judgments reflects, for one thing, the variety of critical tempers in different ages. It is also apparent, from the distance between the judgments of a single critic, Dr. Johnson, that the variety is partly in Dryden and in his poetry. There is even remarkable variety within Dr. Johnson's catalogue of faults: "He had not yet learned [when he wrote *Astraea Redux,* 1660], indeed he never learned well, to forbear the improper use of mythology." ". . . There is so much likeness in the initial comparison that there is no illustration. As a king would be lamented, Eleonora was lamented." "The comparison of the Chancellor to the Indies leaves all resemblance too far behind it."[1]* And, moreover, it is not all a matter of Dryden's variousness in kind and method, but also of the variation in the quality of his poetry. As Mark Van Doren has observed: "Dryden is as unequal as any English poet who has written voluminously."[2]

Dryden's variousness and inequality will no doubt answer for a good deal of the apparent jangling of critical judgments. The fable

Notes for the Introduction are on page xiii.

of the blind men and the elephant does apply. But Dryden, who had a way of writing scrupulously different styles in carefully differentiated kinds of poetry, had also a way of modulating and adjusting together some apparently antithetical virtues or opposed vices of style. He had, for example, a way of writing that, from a baldly statistical point of view, abounded in similes while it was engaged in a process which produced metaphors. He had, as T. S. Eliot has observed, the ability to state immensely. The critical judgments, taken all together, hint at richness. One way of illuminating Dryden's capacity is to study his imagery.

An approach to Dryden's imagery by way of a study of representative examples of his nondramatic poetry is a ready way, and seems a sound method, of shedding some light on the kinds of imagery characteristically used by Dryden and the range in his methods of employing imagery. There are obvious advantages in limiting the subject matter of this study so that the poetry considered can be studied in some detail, but it has seemed equally obvious that the basis in the poetry must be broad enough to include at least an approximation of the range in the kinds of Dryden's poetry. The prologues and epilogues constitute by themselves a considerable body of poetry (there are about ninety-five of them), and they are poems that enjoyed in Dryden's own day considerable reputation. They are the most convenient material for a study of how he used imagery when he was writing poetry that was to be spoken in the theater. They also offer the means to a survey of the uses of imagery where the subject matter is highly contemporary, social, and perilously evanescent. And they happen to offer the range from praise to blame of a nondeliberative rhetoric, with a series of examples of the positive mode of amplification located in the Oxford prologues and a host of examples of the negative mode of amplification located in the London prologues. *Religio Laici* is included as an example of a middle kind of poem written in the deliberative style, and provides the base for studying imagery as related to argument. Argument in verse was one of Dryden's special talents and frequent occupations, and *Religio Laici*, so characteristic of the kind of poetic performance that has earned the designation "poetry of statement," is a good place to study the amount and kind and function of imagery in association with a middle style. *Absalom and Achitophel* is included as an example of the narrative poem with affinities both to history and to epic. This poem, a generally admired example of Dryden's capacity in occasional and quasi-official poetry, offers an inviting avenue of approach to the study of imagery applied to the permanent etching of a group of public figures and public events, and of imagery as a way of admitting the heroic style. Finally there is Dryden's performance in elegy and ode to be considered; the elegy *To the Memory of Mr. Oldham* and the ode *To the Pious Memory of . . . Mrs. Anne Killigrew* have been selected as examples, the former because it is a notable instance of restrained and limited elegiac compliment written in a style that seems almost akin to that of *Religio Laici,* almost deliberative rather than demonstrative, and the latter because it is an obvious example of the unleashed, amplifying, soaring kind of compliment. There is a range within the rhetoric of praise, and the relation of imagery to this range deserves to be explored.

Although this study of Dryden's imagery has not been conceived primarily as a chronological survey of his whole career as a poet, it has seemed worth while to discuss at some length major examples of his early and late poetry in order that the reader may have, in the end, some sense of the full sweep of Dryden's poetic career. Accordingly, the first chapter essays an account of representative early poems, and the sixth chapter attempts to do the same for poetry of Dryden's last decade.

NOTES

1. *Lives of the Poets,* ed. G. B. Hill (3 vols., Oxford, 1905), I, 427, 441, 429.
2. *John Dryden: A Study of His Poetry* (3rd ed.; New York: Henry Holt and Co., 1946), p. 30; now with same pagination in the "Midland Books" paperback series (Bloomington: Indiana University Press, 1960).

I

An Apprenticeship in Praise

S Mark Van Doren remarks in his influential survey of Dryden's poetry, "no critic has felt that he could afford to commend Dryden in general without proving that he had taken into account the worst of him in particular."[1]* There is, however, something defensive and seemingly ungenerous about such a procedure, though a critic must establish his own credit in order to establish the credit of the poet. The procedure may seem to be at odds with Dryden's own conception that critics are properly the defenders of poets and the main business of the critic is to exhibit the excellences of the poet. Yet it is certain that to understand Dryden's excellences we must explore his variousness, confronting that variety when it is sad as well as when it is rich and happy. Dryden was, as Congreve remarked, an improving poet to the last, and many of his later improvements are achieved by setting earlier mediocrities in a new key or transposing a vain extravagance into a new context where it is filled with meaning.

The circumstance that Dryden began as a poet in an extended series of poems of compliment, many of them addressed to rulers of state and to major public events, is of the first importance as a groundwork for his subsequent development. In 1649 he produced his elegy *Upon the Death of the Lord Hastings;* in 1650 his complimentary lines *To John Hoddesdon, on His Divine Epigrams;* in 1658 his *Heroique Stanzas to the Glorious Memory of Cromwell;* in 1660 *Astraea Redux,* celebrating the return of Charles II; in the same year the complimentary poem *To My Honored Friend, Sir Robert Howard;* in 1661 *To His Sacred Majesty, A Panegyrick on*

*Notes for this chapter are on page 19.

His Coronation; in 1662 *To My Lord Chancellor,* celebrating the statesmanship of Edward Hyde, Earl of Clarendon; in the same year a complimentary epistle *To My Honored Friend, Dr. Charleton;* probably in 1663 the lines addressed *To the Lady Castlemaine, upon Her Incouraging His First Play;* and in 1666 (published 1667) *Annus Mirabilis: The Year of Wonders, 1666,* a poem that considerably exceeds the frame of the usual poem of compliment but that is important in this series for its attempt to bring king and people together within the same focus of compliment.

Under the lengthened shadow of Dr. Johnson's well-known strictures on obsequious flattery of the great, it has been more the custom to deplore the motives than to explore the style and content of these poems. Dr. Johnson, in a characteristically pungent passage, managed at once to acknowledge and to lament Dryden's facility in this vein: ". . . in the meanness and servility of hyperbolical adulation I know not whether, since the days in which the Roman emperors were deified, he has been ever equalled, except by Afra Behn in an address to Eleanor Gwyn. When once he has undertaken the task of praise he no longer retains shame in himself, nor supposes it in his patron. As many odoriferous bodies are observed to diffuse perfumes from year to year without sensible diminution of bulk or weight, he appears never to have impoverished his mint of flattery by his expences, however lavish. He had all forms of excellence, intellectual and moral, combined in his mind, with endless variation; and when he had scattered on the hero of the day the golden shower of wit and virtue, he had ready for him, whom he wished to court on the morrow, new wit and virtue with another stamp. Of this kind of meanness he never seems to decline the practice, or lament the necessity: he considers the great as entitled to encomiastick homage, and brings praise rather as a tribute than a gift, more delighted with the fertility of his invention than mortified by the prostitution of his judgment. It is indeed not certain that on these occasions his judgment much rebelled against his interest. There are minds which easily sink into submission, that look on grandeur with undistinguishing reverence, and discover no defect where there is elevation of rank and affluence of riches."[2] It seems proper to urge a discrimination of the biographical judgments involved in Johnson's comment. It is difficult at our distance in time to judge Dryden's motives, and the

2

motives are inessential to a judgment of the poetry. If the poetry offers lines that are sounding brass or tinkling cymbal, we may well discover their hollowness by confronting them squarely without resort to the indirection of biographical inference. Men with the best motives in the world have written execrable poetry, and that men with execrable motives may yet write well is an unpalatable fact that critics must swallow in their progress toward familiarity with what W. H. Auden calls "the treason of all clerks." In his poem *In Memory of W. B. Yeats,* Auden puts the point succinctly:

Time that is intolerant
Of the brave and innocent,
And indifferent in a week
To a beautiful physique,

Worships language and forgives
Everyone by whom it lives;
Pardons cowardice, conceit,
Lays its honours at their feet.[3]

The earliest poem in the series of complimentary pieces, the elegy *Upon the Death of the Lord Hastings,* is comparatively free from the tincture of suspect motives of policy and advantage. It is, it should be remembered, a schoolboy's poem, and the conjecture is reasonable that it was produced, along with other poems by Westminster boys that appeared in the Hastings volume, under the direction of the famous master, Dr. Busby. The poems by Dryden's schoolfellows were in Latin and imitated Latin models. Dryden's poem, in English, is altogether more ambitious, and Busby was apparently willing, with some natural granted and expected allowance, to have it stand beside the work of Denham, Marvell, Herrick, and Brome. The formal plan and capacity of the poem have been admirably set forth by Miss Ruth Wallerstein, who, after careful study of all the poems in the Hastings volume, finds Dryden's elegy no mean production, even in such company. Miss Wallerstein remarks: ". . . he shows a far deeper sense of the elegy as a formal poetic genre than anyone who wrote for the King volume except Milton, and than any other contributors to the Hastings volume except Denham and Herrick and Marvell." Later she says: "Dryden's *Hastings* has not the personal and emotional tone to win our interest as does, say, Shelley's early poetry: but in scope, in ordonnance, in its selections and rejections, in its wonderful sense of artistic purpose, it is the prophecy of a major poet and of a new age."[4] Miss Wallerstein recognizes that the poem is callow and in some ways naïvely imitative, revealing in its stiffness that the poetic talent here displayed is only beginning to exercise itself. But she is not led astray into fixed contemplation of certain faults of style which have stuck in the eyes of many earlier critics. Dr. Johnson, of course, boggled at the conceits of the poem, especially those having to do with smallpox. Scott, in one motion, recognized and deplored the antecedents of some of the stylistic features of the poem which he calls ". . . a servile imitation of the conceits of Cleveland and the metaphysical wit of Cowley, exerted in numbers hardly more harmonious than those of Donne."[5]

The poem has drawn fire not only from Scott but also from Mark Van Doren for its tunelessness. Van Doren says: "Metrically it was chaos. Gray remarked to Mason that it seemed the work of a man who had no ear and might never have any."[6] With respect to the conceits and with respect to metrics there are some observations to be made not more out of charity than out of simple fairness. A poet of eighteen does not usually invent at one blow a new style; he employs the style or styles available to him. Dryden did not originate the bad conceit; he adopted a conceited style that had reached the stage of decay. He did not have to invent his conceits on smallpox. Cartwright had written on the subject of smallpox, and other elegists of Hastings, as Miss Wallerstein points out, found the topic inevitable and went at it in the received style. Needham wrote:

> Those eyes which Hymen hop'd should light his Torch,
> Aethereal flames of Fevers now do scorch,
> And *envious Pimples* too dig Graves apace,
> To bury all the Glories of his face.[7]

Charles Cotton wrote:

> Bathe him in Tears, till there appear no trace
> Of those sad Blushes in his lovely face:
> Let there be in't of Guilt no seeming sence,
> Nor other Colour then of Innocence.[8]

The roughness of Dryden's numbers is, as Scott recognized, not without example. A comparable roughness can be found in many passages of Donne's *Anniversaries.* There is something about the method by which Dryden's poem moves that imitates a characteristic method of Donne's, and there is something about that method of movement that entails roughness. The method is interrogative and argumentative, querying and postulating, leading up to conceits by way of questions, using the conceits as postulates and deriving corollaries. A pseudo logic is developed to force the reader to follow the conceit, and since the primary objective of the poet is to tie the mind of the reader effectively to the development and progress of the conceit, no exterior considerations of tuneful harmony or smooth movement can enter in; the only appropriate harmony in such poetry is one which does not get in the way of but enforces the conceit. Meter is cast upon a Procrustean bed, wracked and torn, and is most whole when most torn provided only that the conceit itself justifies the torture. It is perfectly clear that Dryden's conceit—and, we may add, the conceit as Dryden received it—seldom justifies the torture:

> Was there no milder way but the Small Pox,
> The very Filth'ness of *Pandora's* Box?
> So many Spots, like *naeves,* our *Venus* soil?
> One Jewel set off with so many a Foil?
> Blisters with pride swell'd; which th'row's flesh did sprout
> Like Rose-buds, stuck i' th' Lily-skin about.
> Each little Pimple had a Tear in it,
> To wail the fault its rising did commit:
> Who, Rebel-like, with their own Lord at strife,
> Thus made an Insurrection 'gainst his Life.
> Or were these Gems sent to adorn his Skin,
> The Cab'net of a richer Soul within?
>
> (ll. 53-64; I, 4C; I, 2K)

The point to be made here is that the conceited metaphysical style at its best is closely allied to a very special and domineering treatment of metrics. If one grants that the metaphysical style was irretrievably sinking under the sheer weight of too many bad conceits, then one must concede that the *raison d'être* of a particular treatment of metrics was disappearing. In Dryden's progress as a poet, the rejection of the conceit and the rejection of harsh numbers went hand in hand.

Before leaving the subject of Dryden's metrics in this poem and proceeding to consideration of the poem as opening the vein of compliment, I want to include a suggestion offered by Miss Wallerstein because it is pertinent not only to this poem but also to subsequent developments in Dryden's early poetry which this study attempts to shed some light on: "It is true that the versification lacks that resonance which 'fortune rarely gives the young.' But Scott, reading it with an ear attuned to the heroic couplet, saw only its defect. To me the rhythm suggests a probable attempt to mediate between speech rhythms and the formal movement of the new couplet. If so, it follows Denham, and it is Dryden's first try at the principle which was to create his great verse."[9]

When one considers this elegy's method of creating its focus of praise, one notices, of course, the employment of conceit and paradox to define and elevate the figure at the center of the poem. But besides the familiar Donnian method of "proving" the tremendous consequences of a death and thereby establishing the magnitude and quality of the deceased, there is a parallel procedure, or the beginning of a parallel procedure. Mixed in with the paradoxical method there are the materials of a more straightforward substantiation of the focus of praise:

> O had he di'd of old, how great a strife
> Had been, who from his Death should draw their Life?
> Who should, by one rich draught, become what ere
> *Seneca, Cato, Numa, Caesar,* were:
> Learn'd, Vertuous, Pious, Great; and have by this
> An universal *Metempsuchosis.*
>
> (ll. 67-72; I, 4-5C; I, 2K)

The alignment of a series of classical exemplars of qualities which in the next line are enumerated in a parallel series is here subsumed within the conceit of metempsychosis, a conceit familiar in Donne, but the foundation is laid in the neat ranking and equation for an analogic structure independent of the conceit, and the later Dryden is full of allusive analogies to classical figures which, without the schoolboyish enumeration of the appropriate qualities, make the name serve as a compact metaphor of a quality, and link the name by overt simile to the particular focus of praise. The classical names become, for Dryden, designations of the many provinces in the moral realm, and the full range of ethical discriminations is ordered by way of the models. Theological figures and conceits, such as the one which in the passage above embraces the ethical evaluation, are suppressed, and the appearance of theology or metaphysics in a poem comes to be managed in a different fashion.

The Hastings elegy makes it clear that Dryden, at this stage, was uncertain about the couplet. His uncertainty persisted for some time and expressed itself in several experiments in quatrains, testing the usefulness of the example offered by Davenant's *Gondibert*. As a result, we have Dryden's *Heroique Stanzas* (for Cromwell) and his *Annus Mirabilis* in quatrains. It seems probable, though not strictly demonstrable, that uncertainty about the conceit and uncertainty about the couplet went hand in hand and were quite significantly related. In the Hastings elegy he was employing the couplet at one remove from Donne's manner and at several removes from his own ultimate practice. Donne sometimes concluded a movement with a heavily end-stopped first line of a couplet and began anew with the second line. This Dryden did not do in his elegy, but most of the other devices for tailoring the verse to the measure of the conceit Dryden did follow. He employed run-over lines casting a word into a distinct, emphatic prominence at the beginning of the second line:

> Must all these ag'd Sires in one Funeral
> Expire?
>
> (ll. 73-74; I, 5C; I, 2K)

He hammered out lines in which the stresses wrestled down the iambic norm while the words themselves, common words, were deliberately played at tug-of-war with the dignified, solemn side of the elegy's complex of feeling and tone, producing a not very happy version of the metaphysical inclusion of extremes of language and feeling:

> Must Drunkards, Lechers, spent with Sinning, live
> With such helps as Broths, Possits, Physick give?
> None live, but such as should die?
>
> (ll. 85-87; I, 5C; I, 3K)

He employed sentence structures that listened to a drum different from that heard by the line or couplet. He even ended a sentence and started another in the middle of a line, as Donne sometimes did, and generally made grammatical divisions disruptive of line and couplet:

7

Must *Vertue* prove *Death's* Harbinger? Must She,
With him expiring, feel Mortality?
Is *Death* (Sin's wages) Grace's now? shall Art
Make us more Learned, onely to depart?
If Merit be Disease, if Vertue Death;
To be Good, Not to be; who'd then bequeath
Himself to Discipline? Who'd not esteem
Labour a Crime, Study Self-murther deem?

(ll. 5-12; I, 3C; I, 1K)

But that transcends thy skill; thrice happie all,
Could we but prove thus Astronomical.

(ll. 41-42; I, 4C; I, 2K)

He is far from any steady idea of a studied use of caesura to exploit the various balances of a line and, of course, farther still from the interanimation of half-lines within a full, complex, formally structured couplet. Now and again, perhaps, the conceited manner is employed with a stiff neatness that suggests the conciseness and compactness of lines in some of Dryden's later couplets:

Beauty and Learning thus together meet,
To bring a *Winding* for a *wedding-sheet?*

(ll. 3-4; I, 3C; I, 1K)

The Nations sin hath drawn that Veil, which shrouds
Our Day-spring in so sad benighting Clouds.

(ll. 49-50; I, 4C; I, 2K)

But he is not trying to achieve any sustained or frequent effects of balance or antithesis, and the ironies and distinctions as well as the accumulation and power of his later couplets can scarcely be anticipated here.

Almost ten years later in the *Heroique Stanzas* to Cromwell Dryden wrote quatrains (rhymed *abab*) of astonishing smoothness. As Mark Van Doren remarks: "In this poem . . . Dryden wielded with positive assurance a mighty line which was much his own."[10] The evidence all but compels acceptance of Van Doren's conjecture that the intervening period must have been devoted to a good deal of practice in verse. Neither the lines to Hoddesdon (1650) nor those to Honor Dryden (1655) prepare us for the competence of the *Heroique*

Stanzas. I am not sure, as Professor Van Doren seems to be, that we need to suppose a great *variety* of experiment, but to do without the supposition of very considerable poetic practice seems difficult. Of course, we must remember the element of deliberation in the rough meter of the Hastings elegy; Dryden did not there choose to show how smoothly and yet powerfully he could handle a line, but wrote purposefully rugged verse in a received style. We must not fall into the error of seeing a sheer difference in competence where the issue is complicated by a deliberate difference in style and method.

The conceit appears in the *Heroique Stanzas,* but remarkably tempered and subdued—subdued, that is, to the verse pattern. The striking feature here is the frequent successful employment of the method of overt analogy, the appropriate, carefully cut and limited, but finely illuminating comparison. First, to illustrate what is now happening to the conceit, we may consider an example such as that in the twenty-seventh stanza:

> When such *Heröique Vertue* Heav'n sets out,
> The Starrs like *Commons* sullenly obey;
> Because it draines them when it comes about,
> And therefore is a taxe they seldome pay.
>
> (ll. 105-08; I, 14-15C; I, 11K)

The conceit here is swiftly and economically generated, developed, and completed. The short simile, *like Commons,* quickly introduces the full spread of the conceit, yoking the astronomical to the political figure, and *taxe* in the last line intensifies by its specification the extravagance implicit in the conceit. The conceit, however, does not dominate the verse structure; the stanza that presents the conceit retains its integrity. The syntactical structure employed to present the conceit is so contrived that each verse line carries a straightforward and distinct part of the statement: statement, consequence, explanation of consequence, conclusion (*When,* first line; [*then*], second line; *Because,* third line; *therefore,* fourth line). The fluidity and sustained movement of this quatrain are prophetic; they are virtues effectively capitalized when Dryden attains his matured couplet style.

The smooth management of the full-dress conceit is important, but more important in the general movement of the poem is the easy but apt analogy, either empirical or conventional. There are a great many of these similes, varying in length from the minimal two words to two lines. The poem gets under way with one of these figures in its opening stanza:

> And now 'tis time; for their Officious haste,
> Who would before have born him to the sky,
> Like *eager Romans* ere all Rites were past
> Did let too soon the *sacred Eagle* fly.
>
> (ll. 1-4; I, 11C; I, 6K)

Another simile, in the sixth stanza, illustrates the smooth accommodation of the empirical and the traditional, gliding from the empirical image for wars to the conventional *sun* symbol of the ruler:

> And Warr's like mists that rise against the Sunne
> Made him but greater seem, not greater grow.
>
> (ll. 23-24; I, 11C; I, 7K)

The figure is developed without impeding the verbal movement, which remains clear and strong. The same sustained verbal movement can be seen in the two comparisons in the thirteenth stanza:

> Swift and resistlesse through the Land he past
> Like that bold *Greek* who did the East subdue;
> And made to battails such Heroick haste
> As if on wings of victory he flew.
>
> (ll. 49-52; I, 12C; I, 8K)

Variety and fertility characterize the images applied to Cromwell, variety rather than managed pattern. A partial cue to the imagery of the poem is provided in the initial suggestion of a Roman apotheosis. Much of the imagery and illustration that follow is drawn from classical figures and customs, both Greek and Roman, and the astronomical comparisons, of which there are quite a few, seem to be initiated and prepared for by the ceremonial apotheosis enskying the soul of the hero at the beginning.

Astraea Redux, less than two years later (1660), celebrating the return of Charles II, shows an important development in the application of imagery and allusion to praise. Indeed, the poem is in such a variety of ways significant of things to come that it is a convenient base for a number of illustrations looking toward Dryden's later technique.

The pungency of Dr. Johnson's attack on what he called Dryden's facility in flattery has perhaps drawn attention away from the fact that a structure of compliment can be a burden of obligation. The very excesses, the most ambitious flights of praise creating the heroic model, while they elevate the person praised to a lofty pinnacle, can have also the effect of exposing him. And Dryden, when he had brought the process of compliment to a certain altitude, liked suddenly to disclose that an atmosphere rarefied is also difficult to survive in and that the light of such a region, while it can create a transfiguring nimbus, can also search and probe with brilliant shafts. So, for example, what this poem has made of Charles' exile, a learning by suffering, is advanced as a commitment for the future:

> Inur'd to suffer ere he came to raigne
> No rash procedure will his actions stain.
> To bus'ness ripened by digestive thought
> His future rule is into Method brought.
>
> (ll. 87-90; I, 24C; I, 18K)

Just beneath the surface of compliment are perilous rocks upon which kings have foundered. The poem takes cognizance of the peculiar perils to the king of restoration after the kingless Commonwealth, restoration to a throne which the people had but recently discovered they had power to shake, and possibly these lines are also an implicit recognition of regal errors in the recent past. All this is carried off as a compliment, yet a real and present peril affecting the conduct of kingship at this particular juncture is being recognized, and just back of the veil of compliment the lines present a warning face.

A similar grave demand emerges from the light of compliment in a passage where the movement of praise is near its summit and powerfully ascending:

> And welcome now (*Great Monarch*) to your own;
> Behold th' approaching cliffes of *Albion*;
> It is no longer Motion cheats your view,
> As you meet it, the Land approacheth you.
> The Land returns, and in the white it wears
> The marks of penitence and sorrow bears.
> But you, whose goodness your discent doth show,
> Your Heav'nly Parentage and earthly too;
> By that same mildness which your Fathers Crown

11

Before did ravish, shall secure your own.
Not ty'd to rules of Policy, you find
Revenge less sweet then a forgiving mind.
Thus when th' Almighty would to *Moses* give
A sight of all he could behold and live;
A voice before his entry did proclaim
Long-Suff'ring, Goodness, Mercy in his Name.
Your Pow'r to Justice doth submit your Cause,
Your Goodness only is above the Laws;
Whose rigid letter while pronounc'd by you
Is softer made. . . .

(ll. 250-69; I, 29C; I, 22-23K)

The passage is certainly not wanting in compliment, hyperbole, and the most honorific comparison. At the advent of the *Great Monarch* the land itself moves penitently toward him. The monarch is like God in the proclaimed virtues which herald his approach. But the virtues become conditions of the return. It is *goodness* that is the sign of the lineal and true king. It is *mildness* that will secure the throne. It is a time for *a forgiving mind* to rise superior to a mean and factional policy of revenge. God Himself, in His appearance to Moses, was proclaimed in terms of *Long-Suff'ring, Goodness, Mercy*. The king's power is represented as submitting itself to justice (and it is, after all, the return of Astraea which the poem has for its subject); it is the king's goodness, not the king's power that is above the laws. A king is a true king and god-like when his character tempers the severity rather than enforces the rigor of the laws. The whole pattern of compliment thus has a tempering and restricting undertone; even the conceit which puts the land's submission and penance at the extreme and seems to abase the people at the advent of the great monarch has this undertone:

As you meet it, the Land approacheth you.

The conditional possibility latent in *As* perhaps reflects the fact that the King's return, thoroughly welcome though it was to almost all the strife-wearied people, was not besought by a groveling popular submission but was based on terms. The Declaration of Breda, worked out by Clarendon, had made it possible for Charles to return without the assistance of foreign arms. The king moving toward the land and the land toward the king make an accurate image of the

12

rapprochement. *Th' approaching cliffes of Albion* are white in token of penance, but as they are cliffs they may also carry the suggestion of the difficulties that attend monarchy in this realm.

The method of extending and at the same time limiting is to be remarked not only as applied to the character of the king, but also as applied to the narrative action in which the royal figure is engaged. Poetry, as Aristotle observed, differs from history; history is occupied with particulars, whereas the poetic account constitutes an action that is universal. This difference is clearly visible in Dryden's poetry throughout his long career because his poetry is so frequently occasional and takes its rise from immediate historical events. Consequently the process of transmuting historical sequence into poetic action is a prominent feature of his poetry. It is the explicitness of the historical material that makes the process peculiarly visible, and there are occasions when the historical material is so bulky and unwieldy that it proves intransigent to the myth-making power with the result that the transmutation is never satisfactorily completed. Dryden did, however, develop an extraordinary ability to assimilate complex sequences and tangles of history; *Absalom and Achitophel* is an astonishing example of resourcefulness in turning history into myth. In *Astraea Redux* the outlines of the typical procedure may be observed.

There is, first, a titular myth—the return of the goddess of justice, Astraea brought back. In this case the titular myth is classical. Second, the content of the myth as it is developed in the poem is both classical and Christian, or biblical. (In the case of *Absalom and Achitophel* the titular myth is biblical, the content both classical and Christian.) The goddess of justice who resided on earth during the Saturnian golden age was driven out by the wickedness and impiety of the brazen and iron ages. As the constellation Virgo, the goddess with her sword and scales has taken her place in the heavens. The return of the goddess to earth will occur when, in the revolution of time, the golden age returns. Such a renewal of time had been attributed to the reign of Augustus, and Dryden completes the cycle in his poem by presenting the return of Charles as the beginning of a new Augustan age. The mythical fabric is enhanced with a variety of classical material, much of it fairly close to the myth of Astraea. So, for example, Charles' exile is compared to the flight of Jove, and the

English rebellion becomes the revolt of the Titans in which "bold Typhoeus" violated heaven and forced Jove to flee. "The rabble" are compared, in their blindness, to the Cyclops, another of the giant brood. These classical materials are drawn principally from Virgil's *Fourth Eclogue,* or *Pollio,* from the sixth book of the *Aeneid,*[11] from the first and thirteenth books of Ovid's *Metamorphoses,* and possibly from Hesiod's *Theogony.* Virgil's *Pollio* is here, as so frequently in seventeenth- and eighteenth-century treatments of the classical golden age, a crucial source because it is so closely analogous to the Christian Messianic tradition, and because the connection had long been recognized not only as a literary parallel but as a mystical linking of Christian and classical Sibylline prophecy. The argument prefacing Dryden's translation of the *Pollio* concludes with this statement: "Many of the Verses are translated from one of the Sybils, who prophesie of our Saviour's Birth" (II, 887K). Accordingly Dryden's treatment of the cyclical myth of the golden age is conventional in its admission of Christian material. For the phase of banishment Dryden uses Astraea's and Jove's exiles as the classical analogues of Charles' exile, and for the biblical analogues he uses David's exile, and Adam's banishment from paradise:

> Thus banish'd *David* spent abroad his time,
> When to be Gods Anointed was his Crime.
>
> (ll. 79-80; I, 24C; I, 18K)
>
> Such is not *Charles* his too too active age,
> Which govern'd by the wild distemper'd rage
> Of some black Star infecting all the Skies,
> Made him at his own cost like *Adam* wise.
>
> (ll. 111-14; I, 25C; I, 19K)

Dryden's account of the return, filled with the millenary suggestions of the *Pollio,* becomes quite explicitly Messianic in its imagery, employing a celestial omen that Charles' contemporaries had connected with him as the pivot on which to turn to a strong allusion to the birth of Christ, the Savior and the divine King:

> That Star that at your Birth shone out so bright
> It stain'd the duller Suns Meridian light,
> Did once again its potent Fires renew
> Guiding our eyes to find and worship you.
>
> (ll. 288-91; I, 30C; I, 23K)

14

A more explicitly Messianic passage is the following:

> Heav'n would no bargain for its blessings drive
> But what we could not pay for, freely give.
> The Prince of Peace would like himself confer
> A gift unhop'd without the price of war.
> Yet as he knew his blessings worth, took care
> That we should know it by repeated pray'r;
> Which storm'd the skies and ravish'd *Charles* from thence
> As Heav'n it self is took by violence.
>
> (ll. 137-44; I, 26C; I, 19K)

The sequence of the mythical action is supported by a pattern of imagery. The initial scene of disorder is presented by "black Clouds," furious "Winds," "Stiff gales," "some black Star infecting all the Skies." The restoration of order is characterized by the dispersion of "Those Clouds that overcast your Morne"; the winds now calmed and, in their joy and submission, even too faint; the star of Charles' birth renewing its fires; the land, returning, wearing white; and "times whiter series . . . /Which in soft Centuries shall smoothly run." Not only the extreme conditions, but also the transition from one to the other is reflected in the imagery and managed with special adroitness in two passages:

> Well might the Ancient Poets then confer
> On Night the honour'd name of *Counseller,*
> Since struck with rayes of prosp'rous fortune blind
> We light alone in dark afflictions find.
>
> (ll. 93-96; I, 24C; I, 18K)

> Yet as wise Artists mix their colours so
> That by degrees they from each other go,
> Black steals unheeded from the neighb'ring white
> Without offending the well cous'ned sight:
> So on us stole our blessed change; while we
> Th' effect did feel but scarce the manner see.
> Frosts that constrain the ground, and birth deny
> To flow'rs, that in its womb expecting lye,
> Do seldom their usurping Pow'r withdraw,
> But raging floods pursue their hasty thaw:
> Our thaw was mild, the cold not chas'd away
> But lost in kindly heat of lengthned day.
>
> (ll. 125-36; I, 25C; I, 19K)

This pattern of imagery is consistent with both classical and Christian models. The storms and the black star are close to the tempests and black fire of Virgil's *Aeneid;* black fire is fire that comes from below and is contrasted by Virgil to the flashing fire of Jove's thunderbolt that comes from above. Dryden affirms the suggestion of hellish dominion in the period of disorder by presenting also a Christian version of it; "Legion" is the image he uses for those who have possessed the "once sacred house." The allusion to Night as counselor is classical and together with the reference to blindness may suggest the great exemplars of sight out of blindness, Tiresias and King Oedipus, but as the second passage develops the transition from black to white, from darkness to light, the change is capped with a Messianic allusion, and thus the Isaiahan prophecies are also drawn into the background. The title of the Messiah here is the Prince of Peace, which occurs in the sequence "Counselor . . . the Prince of Peace" (Isaiah 9:6). The imagery may derive its color, then, from Isaiahan as well as classical shadings; the transition from dark to light, for example, is part of the Messianic vision: "The people that walked in darkness have seen a great light: they that dwell in the land of the shadow of death, upon them hath the light shined" (Isaiah 9:2). And the picture of the restored king's government, in its closeness to Virgil's *Pollio,* is also close to Isaiah; Dryden writes:

Abroad your Empire shall no Limits know,
But like the Sea in boundless Circles flow.

(ll. 298-99; I, 30C; I, 23K)

Such lines are associated with a generalized prophetic strain; the prophet's version is familiar: "Of the increase of his government and peace there shall be no end" (Isaiah 9:7).

The whole pattern of classical and biblical allusion which creates the special myth of this poem ranges from very overt references to much more tacit correspondences and parallels. Since the more tacit sort of reference is so important to Dryden's poetic method throughout his career, it may be well to cite an additional example of this device. It has already been suggested that his general pattern of imagery supporting the mythical action can be paralleled in the *Aeneid;* the presentation of Charles, the chief actor, is also managed in a way to suggest occasionally the heroic figure of Aeneas. The section from line 43 to line 58 makes Charles a Roman figure, suffering for himself and his people, enduring with fortitude the vicissitudes of storms at sea. The amassing of details contributes to the effect, but the contour of the language clinches the suggestion:

> He toss'd by Fate, and hurried up and down,
> Heir to his Fathers Sorrows, with his Crown,
> Could tast no sweets of youths desired Age,
> But found his life too true a Pilgrimage.

(ll. 51-54; I, 23C; I, 17K)

Toss'd by Fate echoes Virgilian language and constructions—*fato profugus* and *vi superum . . . iactatus*—that are the signature of Aeneas' trials by sea.[12]

Perhaps the most significant general conclusion that emerges from close attention to the imagery and diction of this early poem is that in his poems of compliment Dryden was, from the beginning, occupied with the accommodation of the classical and the Christian images of the hero. This problem of creating the hero along the lines of two traditions had been confronted by Chaucer in *The Knight's Tale,* by Spenser in *The Faerie Queene,* and was to be faced anew by Milton in *Paradise Lost.* The conceptions of the convergences and divergences of the two traditions varied from age to age and from poet to poet; in the seventeenth century Puritanism gave a new acuteness to the problem, and in Milton it is the sense of divergence that grows sharper and more insistent, with the result that instead of an accommodation of two heroic images there is, in *Paradise Lost,* supersession of an older heroic image by a new image of the Christian hero.[13]

It is interesting to find Dryden, much later in his career, in the dedication of his translation of Virgil, saying: "I must acknowledge that *Virgil* in Latine, and *Spencer* in English, have been my Masters" (III, 1048K). The context of this expression of indebtedness suggests that Dryden was speaking primarily of a debt to Spenser in matters of versification, but it seems reasonable to suggest that his awareness of Spenser probably also included awareness of Spenser's way of accommodating the classical and Christian heroic images. It is, in fact, hard to imagine a seventeenth-century English poet aware of his tradition who would not be aware of the problem or who would not find that he had to work out his own ways of meeting the problem. It happened that Dryden met the problem early and frequently on the rather special ground of the poem of compliment addressed to public figures. Consequently it was public virtue of which he had to make the image. Besides the strong classical tradition which had developed the genre and continued strongly to influence its form, there was the fact that heroic images in the mold of chiefs of government were more easily drawn from classical than from Christian sources. On this ground—the ground of compliment to public leaders—it would have been hard to do without the classical tradition. What he could not easily do without, Dryden proceeded emphatically to do with, and probably the will behind this emphasis derives strength, and, in Dryden's case, more and more strength as time goes by, from royalism and anti-Puritanism. The hero is made in the classical as well as the Christian image as a way of disavowing the Puritan rejection of the classical tradition as fabulous, lying, and heathen. *Eikon Basilike* and the martyrology of Charles I were an affront to the Puritan spirit; they were idolatry. This idolatry, this powerful concentration of Christian symbolism upon the figure of the king flourished at the restoration of the martyred king's son. In the poems of compliment, classical imagery of the hero added paganism to idolatry and thus wrote the full royal signature. A rapprochement of classical and Christian, an emphatic mingling of the two in the royal presence, was an expression of the Cavalier spirit.

Much of what has been said here about *Astraea Redux* is anticipatory in mood, looking forward to subsequent developments. The features of this poem which identify it with the early stages of Dryden's development should be acknowledged. Attention certainly should be called to the way he manages couplets in this poem. The obtrusive conceit and the rough Donnian meters of the Hastings elegy have disappeared, but the influence of writing the *Heroique Stanzas* in quatrains in 1658 lingers on in the couplets of *Astraea Redux*. Frequently the unit of organization from a syntactical point of view is quite domineeringly a unit of four lines in which only a mild pause occurs at the end of the first couplet.[14] Dryden has not yet learned to turn around within the strict confines of the couplet; he can do it, but not consistently, not steadily through a long performance. Six years later, in *Annus Mirabilis*, he yields explicitly to the quatrain form of organization—and, with the expansion allowed by the four-line organization, there occurs a renewed efflorescence of the conceit. These hesitations, variations, and uncertainties in his early development are a partial explanation of the fact that Dryden never did completely commit himself to the couplet. He finally developed sanctioned forms to accommodate the tendency that he could not or would not eradicate. One form, for which he claimed Spenser's example, was the Alexandrine or hexameter conclusion of a couplet, and the other, frequently used with an Alexandrine final line, was the triplet. To the end of his career, he remained almost addicted to these devices of expansion. Often he used them powerfully and effectively. It seems a reasonable conjecture, at any rate, that the older Dryden's fondness for these devices had its roots in his early work as a poet, and that the overriding of the couplet in *Astraea Redux* was to be tamed and licensed but never extirpated. It became, in fact, an indulgence that Dryden enjoyed, and what Dryden enjoyed often made his best verse.

NOTES

1. *John Dryden: A Study of His Poetry* (3rd ed., New York, 1946), p. 30.
2. *Lives of the Poets,* ed. G. B. Hill (3 vols., Oxford, 1905), I, 399-400.
3. *The Collected Poetry of W. H. Auden* (New York: Random House, 1945); the phrase "the treason of all clerks" occurs in the last line of the next to last stanza of "At the Grave of Henry James" (p. 130); the quoted stanzas are the second and third of the third part of the poem (p. 50).
4. *Studies in Seventeenth-Century Poetic* (Madison: University of Wisconsin Press, 1950), pp. 115-42.
5. *The Works of John Dryden,* ed. Sir Walter Scott, revised and corrected by George Saintsbury (18 vols., Edinburgh, 1882-93), XI, 93.
6. *John Dryden,* p. 81.
7. Quoted by Wallerstein, p. 126.
8. *Ibid.*
9. *Ibid.,* pp. 135-36.
10. *John Dryden,* p. 82.
11. In Dryden's translation, *Aeneis,* VI, ll. 1073 ff.; III, 1229K.
12. The Aeneas-Charles parallel was drawn by Waller in a poem called *Of the Danger His Majesty . . . Escaped,* ll. 89-93, *The Poems of Edmund Waller,* ed. G. Thorn Drury (2 vols.; London: "The Muses Library," n.d.), I, 1-7.
13. This development in Milton's epic is perhaps analogous to the superseding of the older Homeric heroic image in Virgil's *Aeneid.* Amid the flames of Troy in Book II of the *Aeneid* Aeneas is torn loose from the older image of the hero and made to undertake the exploration and development of a new heroic meaning.
14. For examples of this four-line organization in *Astraea Redux,* see ll. 1-20, 31-34, 51-54, 73-76, 111-14, 131-134, 141-44, 147-50, 153-56, 165-68, 195-98, 211-22, 276-79, 288-91.

II

Prologues and Epilogues

RYDEN's prologues and epilogues provide the ground for a study of the use of imagery in short poems designed to be spoken in public. In his life of Dryden, Dr. Johnson says: "His prologues had such reputation that for some time a play was considered as less likely to be well received if some of his verses did not introduce it."[1]* These poems constitute, for the purposes of this study, an especially useful and convenient body of poetry because chronologically they cover very nearly the full range of Dryden's poetic production, and because they exhibit, in fairly simple form, the use of imagery in two main types, the satiric poem and the poem of compliment. The first prologue was written for his first drama, *The Wild Gallant,* in 1663, and the final epilogue was written in 1700, less than a month before his death, for a performance of Fletcher's play, *The Pilgrim* (as revised by Vanbrugh). The satiric poem appears most frequently in the prologues and epilogues written for London, and the poem of compliment almost exclusively in those for Oxford.[2]

Prologues and epilogues are connected with plays at least by being related to the occasion of the play's performance, and very often they are related not only to the occasion but also directly to the play itself. In classical drama prologues frequently conveyed a certain amount of the exposition of the action about to be exhibited, while epilogues summarized, recapitulated, and commented on the action when it was over. Disengagement of the prologue from the action of the play was accomplished by the comic dramatists, who began to use the forepiece as an independent unit for direct address to the

Notes for this chapter begin on page 53.

public. Shakespeare's prologues and epilogues, though few, are for the most part in the earlier classical manner, closely tied to the action —Ben Jonson's, in the later, comment in general terms on the issues raised by the play or on questions of general moral import bearing on the issues dealt with in the play. Dryden, who wrote about ninety-five such pieces, pushed still farther the estrangement from direct connection with the play. These poems of Dryden's are very often closely connected with the circumstances of a play's performance, some recent event, or the presence of the king and queen, or the date, or the occasion, or the place. Most of them comment on literary, social, and political matters with no direct reference to the play in hand except as point of departure. In Addison's words, "the Prologue and Epilogue were real Parts of the ancient Tragedy; but . . . on the *British* Stage, they are distinct Performances by themselves, Pieces intirely detached from the Play, and no way essential to it."[3] The fact that Dryden himself selected some of his for publication in his poetic *Miscellanies* is good evidence that he regarded these pieces as poetic performances able to stand by themselves and with no necessary relation to the plays.

Once the absence of any necessary connection between these poems and the plays has been stated, however, one may still insist that there often is a connection of a sort that needs to be defined. It is often thematically that the play serves as a point of departure: the prologues and epilogues, particularly the latter, take up a major theme of the play and apply it as commentary to manners and morals, to the state of literature and criticism, to political and religious issues. The epilogue sometimes serves quite overtly to extend the reference of the play, to take up a major theme and pursue it through a circuit of experience, ending with a judgment. Both the forepieces and the afterpieces implicitly insist upon the value and relevance of the play and proceed on the assumption that the work of art, the drama, has a significant relationship to experience. Indeed, these pieces would be impossible without the audience's tacit concurrence in the licensed position of the author, without some sort of acceptance of the assumption that the author is an authoritative spokesman for values. These poems are extensions of the assumptions and values that are involved with the plays, but in the technical sense they are separable from the plays because they are not continuous with the "fables" of the plays.

Dryden's prologues and epilogues comment on a wide variety of matters; they are short, usually not over forty lines in length, and delivered as they were by an actor on the stage, they had to be understood and appreciated by the audience at one hearing.[4] In order to be effective as commentary, poems of this kind need to use sets of strong value and disvalue symbols. These symbols may be traditional or manufactured *ad hoc* within an established framework, but they must be strong, emphatic, and obvious, and the relationships among them must be handled without overt complication. The poet has an obvious advantage if there is a traditional organization of values to which he can refer, within which he can work, and which is sufficiently present in the minds of his audience for them to be easily reminded of it and find it in some degree familiar. As Dryden remarked in the dedication to the *Aeneis*: "A Poet cannot speak too plainly on the Stage: for *Volat irrevocabile verbum;* the sense is lost if it be not taken flying: but what we read alone we have leisure to digest" (III, 1010K).

Dryden's poetic style is basically well equipped to meet these requirements because it is characterized by clarity of syntax and because its major rhetorical device is overt analogy or simile. Some critics, of course, regard these characteristics as belonging especially to good prose, and agree with Arnold's judgment that Dryden and Pope are monuments of our prose. A modern critic writes: "The nature of the change that overtook English poetry between Donne and Dryden is familiar: it is primarily a matter of simplification. At its best, Jacobean poetry unites the maximum of complexity with the maximum of organization, so that no matter how subtle, penetrating, ambiguous, witty, passionate, and imaginative it may be, it is always and in all its parts functional, purposive, organic. When it fails, it fails generally not from overcomplexity, but from too little (or an imperfect) organization. Post-Restoration poetry is much simpler. It is more direct, less profound, and on the whole unambiguous; and in wit, passion, and imaginative quality it is far less concentrated than was English poetry before 1650."[5] It is apparent that for the requirements of the prologue and epilogue, simplicity and directness, a general absence of ambiguity, the qualities depreciated by the critic in the above comparison, are actually merits and quite essential.

22

Moreover, a poetry emphasizing simile makes *relations* explicit, and in the swift establishment of sets of value and disvalue symbols a rhetorical framework which makes relations easily apparent is clearly a desideratum; this kind of poetry will not fail from too little organization.

Besides being a stage finely organized for a variety of logical maneuvers, the couplet becomes, in Dryden's prologues and epilogues, the containing form for a vigorous colloquial vocabulary. This is not to say that all the strength in these pieces is colloquial, for the total vocabulary has other levels and powers as well; the point is that colloquial terms and modes of expression are one of the notable sources of strength. Particularly, the smooth combination of the formality of the couplet with vigorous informal language doubles our consciousness of strength, since we are impressed not only by the racy gestures of words but also by the rhythm and rhyme which command them and unobtrusively set the tune to which they dance. There is an impact of strong language, and then the subtler, more gradually manifested strength of a versification which moves and measures the strongest words, bending usually rather less than one would think necessary to accommodate the most flexible idiomatic expressions. The muscles of a street-fighter occur together with the finished form of a finely trained athlete.

The combination of native strength with sophisticated form is also presented in a different way by the organization of these couplets. Alliteration is rather frequently employed, and is, of course, one way of emphasizing a logical equation or an ironic discrepancy of terms. Yet where the caesura is heavy and roughly medial in the line and where the alliterative linkage is between elements of the two half-lines, a primitive mode of versifying lurks beneath a polished mode. The rugged colloquial language makes the suggestion of a primitive form operate more actively than might otherwise be the case. Here is an example:

> O Poet, damn'd dull Poet, who could prove
> So sensless! to make *Nelly* dye for Love,
> Nay, what's yet worse, to kill me in the prime
> Of *Easter*-Term, in Tart and Cheese-cake time!
> (E, *Tyrannick Love*, ll. 17-20; I, 119K)[6]

and here is another:

23

This jeast was first of t'other houses making,
And, five times try'd, has never fail'd of taking.
For 'twere a shame a Poet shoud be kill'd
Under the shelter of so broad a shield.

(P, Conquest of Granada I, ll. 1-4; I, 128K)

In these examples the hammering alliteration also helps to constitute
the positive, emphatically assertive tone that Dryden often adopted
in these pieces, a driving mode of expression that went on to say to the
hilt what it had to say. A further way of empowering such a tone
was to stretch beyond the couplet to the triplet, piling up phrases
beyond the usual limit and culminating at a greater height, striking
a final effective blow with the third rhyme. Consider, for example,
the following instance in which the triplet accumulates the conditional, and the succeeding (and final) couplet releases the built-up
pressure in one sudden sweep of consequence:

If, notwithstanding all that we can say,
You needs will have your pen'worths of the Play:
And come resolv'd to Damn, because you pay,
   Record it, in memorial of the Fact,
   The first Play bury'd since the Wollen Act.

(P, Oedipus, ll. 32-36; I, 168K)

The imagery of the conclusion in this passage suggests another
facet of Dryden's strength in these pieces. The image, in this case, is
vividly local and contemporary, and the prologues and epilogues
swarm with references and allusions of this sort which, for the immediate audience, would have a striking and vivifying effect. However, the same general principle noticed earlier of combining native
power with formal sophistication appears occasionally in the colloquial imagery of these pieces, and perhaps in no other way are we
offered such a smooth and impressive manifestation of Dryden's
power. Consider, for example, the imagery of these lines:

They talk of Feavours that infect the Brains,
But Non-sence is the new Disease that reigns.
Weak Stomacks with a long Disease opprest,
Cannot the Cordials of strong Wit digest:
Therfore thin Nourishment of Farce ye choose,
Decoctions of a Barly-water Muse:
A Meal of Tragedy wou'd make ye Sick,

Unless it were a very tender Chick.
Some Scenes in Sippets wou'd be worth our time,
Those wou'd go down; some Love that's poach'd in Rime;
If these shou'd fail—
We must lie down, and after all our cost,
Keep Holy-day, like Water-men in Frost,
Whil'st you turn Players on the Worlds great Stage,
And Act your selves the Farce of your own Age.

(P, Loyal General, ll. 20-34; I, 163-64C; I, 205-06K)

Certainly the homely images are piled on; we are fed more and more, more than seems possible. We are stuffed and gorged to the point of disgust, and disgust *is* the point, yet withal so skillfully are we fed, in expressions so finely turned (*Decoctions of a Barly-water Muse; some Love that's poach'd in Rime*), that the wit absorbs its imagery and remains wit. The final achievement, however, is to make the homely, local image open out beyond itself vistas of dignity and seriousness, or, to put the matter another way, to make the common and particular image touch the skirts of a high and general order of poetic symbolism. In a loftier genre, the circumstances here presented of the frustration and defeat of poetry might lead directly to the image of a frozen stream; nevertheless, Dryden, in this lesser genre, activates the same symbolism in a vividly local homely image:

We must lie down, and after all our cost,
Keep Holy-day, like Water-men in Frost.

He comes by way of the Thames watermen to the frozen stream,[7] and the reach of dignity that is opened out by this venture is sustained in the Shakespearean allusion in the final couplet.

The overall management of imagery in these poems combines the immediately flexed muscle of the vivid colloquial images, images characterized by direct and often specifically contemporary impact, with images that draw their power from traditional analogic relationships. Imagery of the former kind acts quickly and boldly in the irrevocable stage moment, the moment in the theater; imagery of the latter kind is quieter, tacitly structural, shaping the form of what happens in the theatrical moment, showing some immediate strength, but transmitting full power only as its systematic analogic relationships are explored and intellectually and meditatively apprehended. We must now attempt to explore this network of systematic analogy, discover-

25

ing the various positions from which it begins, where it characteristically leads, and what lines of argument and patterns of action exist in the sequences and emerge from the whole poetic process.

Every simile is potentially valuative as well as definitive; overt analogies, by affiliating the tenor with an appreciative or depreciative term, are a ready and easily apprehended device for valuing or disvaluing:

> If Souldier-like, he [the poet] may have termes to come.
> (P, *Secret Love*, l. 17; I, 107K)

> He [Shakespeare] Monarch-like gave those his subjects [Fletcher and Jonson] law.
> (P, *The Tempest*, l. 7; I, 116K)

> Some [Englishmen sympathetic to the Dutch] are resolv'd not to find out the Cheat,
> But Cuckold like, love him who does the Feat.
> (P, *Amboyna*, ll. 11-12; I, 151K)

In the first and second examples above, the analogies are appreciative; in the third example the analogy is depreciative.

Since analogy itself is a type of parallelism, the couplet form, with its capacity for presenting emphatic formal parallels, is admirably suited to the forceful presentation of analogy:

> The Spaniel Lover, like a sneaking Fop.
> (E, *Princess of Cleves*, l. 13; I, 382K)

> Guards are illegal, that drive foes away,
> As watchfull Shepherds, that fright beasts of prey.
> (P, *Loyal Brother*, ll. 14-15; I, 247K)

In the first example above the parallelism of half-lines carries the parallelism of the analogy, and the *Spaniel* metaphor assists the economy with which the valuation is accomplished; in the second example the parallelism of whole lines within the couplet carries the parallelism of the analogy.

Clarity of presentation is also served by the couplet form's capacity for antithesis. Value and disvalue can be neatly set off against each other, both ends of the value scale being presented together so that the overt clash enforces the desired differentiation:

> You bore like Hero's, or you brib'd like *Oates*.
> (P, *Albion and Albanius*, l. 6; I, 457K)

Poets, like Lawfull Monarchs, rul'd the Stage,
Till Criticks, like Damn'd Whiggs, debauch'd our Age.

(P, *Loyal Brother*, ll. 1-2; I, 246K)

Since, as the aphorism has it, all things are like and unlike all other things, a poetic style founded on analogy, parallelism, and antithesis has impressive resources for dealing lucidly with its materials.

The examples already cited of valuation by analogy will suggest that appreciation and depreciation are most readily accomplished by employing comparisons which meet something like a *semper et ubique* requirement; the prologues and epilogues cannot afford ingenious comparisons which would require elaborate ratiocination and justification, but must hit upon comparisons of a general kind that will be generally accepted and quickly apprehended as positive or negative in effect. Accordingly there are here no lovers compared to compasses; there are poets compared to lawful monarchs, guards compared to watchful shepherds, people of a particular persuasion and sympathy compared to cuckolds. *Monarchs,* of course, was a value term that had a certain added force for those who were of the king's party in the political conflict of the day, but after the Restoration the conflict raged about the extent of the king's prerogatives or about the religious affiliation of the king, not about the question of whether there was to be a king. *Monarch* was a value term for both parties, whatever their differences about the proper nature of the monarchy. Since the monarch analogy is employed extensively in these poems, it can serve to introduce the discussion of other features of the use of analogy—the application of the same figure to different tenors, and the creation of new figures by analogy or antithesis to a primary value figure.

Monarch appears in similes, and also as metaphor, in various realms. As a monarch can recognize and confirm distinction in commoners and create them knights, so the monarch symbol associated with or made analogous to important terms in a given realm affirms their value, makes them symbols, and in a fairly strict sense creates them knights to function with sanctioned authority within their particular provinces. By a similar process, disvalue terms can be developed within a given realm by associating terms with one or another form of opposition to the monarch or with forces antithetical to a center of authority.

27

In the following examples Oxford occupies a position at the top of the hierarchy of monarch analogies in the aesthetic realm; the university is the sovereign of poets:

> Poets, your [Oxford's] Subjects, have their Parts assign'd
> T' unbend, and to divert their Sovereign's mind.
> <div align="right">(P, <i>Oxford, 1674,</i> ll. 1-2; I, 151C; I, 372K)</div>

Poets, as the *Loyal Brother* example indicates, are themselves lawful monarchs, so that Oxford is elevated to the value position of a *vainqueur du vainqueur.*

Wit is one of the terms that is created a value symbol:

> Let them, who the Rebellion first began,
> To wit, restore the Monarch if they can.
> <div align="right">(P, <i>Kind Keeper,</i> ll. 11-12; I, 175K)</div>

. . . them who the Rebellion first began, used here for aesthetic disvalue, strikes upon strongly resonant surfaces in the political realm, the late deposition and execution of Charles I, and possibly also in the religious realm, since in the political controversy of the day, rebellion against the monarch was conventionally linked, by Dryden and others of Tory sympathies, with Satan's rebellion against God or with Adam's rebellion against the divine command.[8]

Wit is properly a monarch:

> Our Witt as far does forrein wit excell,
> And like a king should in a Pallace dwell.
> <div align="right">(P, <i>Witt without Money,</i> ll. 25-26; I, 143-44C; I, 140K)</div>

It is a bad situation in literature and criticism when *wit* does not reign as monarch:

> But this our age such Authors does afford,
> As make whole Playes, and yet scarce write one word:
> Who in this Anarchy of witt, rob all,
> And what's their Plunder, their Possession call.
> <div align="right">(P, <i>Albumazar,</i> ll. 15-18; I, 141C; I, 141K)</div>

Sense is also a monarch against whose reign *noise* and *madness* are rebels:

> Noise, Madness, all unreasonable Things,
> That strike at Sense, as Rebels do at Kings!
> <div align="right">(P, <i>Loyal General,</i> ll. 14-15; I, 163C; I, 205K)</div>

In the passages here cited, the tenor of the argument is poetry and the stage; aesthetic matters are being discussed by way of political similes and metaphors. It may be said that the flow of valuation is from the similes and metaphors toward the aesthetic terms, but one can scarcely leave it at that because the parallelism has another direction. Valuation is also flowing toward the political terms. The situation may be compared to that in some tidal rivers where, when the tide is coming in, water at the bottom flows in the opposite direction from water at the surface. *Wit* and *sense* are, in themselves, obvious value terms, and being affiliated with the monarch, they have the effect of bolstering the sovereign; "rebels strike at kings as noise, madness, and all unreasonable things strike at sense" is the subterranean echo of the statement about the aesthetic situation. Analogy can be a way of talking about two realms at once. The use of the monarch in analogies strung from one realm to another provides connective tissue for an implicit authoritarian argument. The principle of authority is fortified by connection with a variety of realms. The conventional analogy of the political monarch to God, the divine monarch,[9] is a familiar instance of the interanimative valuation that can be accomplished by analogy between realms:

> When Heav'n made Man, to show the work Divine,
> Truth was his Image, stampt upon the Coin:
> And, when a King is to a God refin'd,
> On all he says and does, he stamps his Mind.
>
> . . . .
>
> He Plights his Faith; and we believe him just;
> His Honour is to Promise, ours to Trust.
> Thus *Britain's* Basis on a Word is laid,
> As by a Word the World it self was made.
>   (E, *Albion and Albanius,* ll. 7-10, 31-34; I, 458K)

> All that our Monarch would for us Ordain,
> Is but t'Injoy the Blessings of his Reign.
> Our Land's an *Eden,* and the Main's our Fence,
> While we Preserve our State of Innocence.
>   (P, *Unhappy Favourite,* ll. 25-28; I, 244K)

In these examples, of course, the tenor of the discussion is political, and value flows primarily from the religious to the political realm.

The monarch similes and metaphors, and similes and metaphors related to them by parallelism or by contrast, are quite pervasive in the prologues and epilogues and appear in various realms of discourse. This practice of repeating analogies of one kind is one of the characteristics that differentiates Dryden's poetic style from a poetic style such as Donne's in which similes and metaphors are much more frequently individual and special, tailored to fit the needs of a particular poetic situation, explored in detail, justified locally, and locally exhausted. Dryden's conventional similes and metaphors are enriched by their repetitions; they become major junction points of a network of analogy. They have the effect, moreover, of creating a chain of command, from the monarch in his highest analogic position —the analogy to God—down to the monarch in such relatively humble analogic positions as analogy to wit or to sense. The importance of the linear connection of such terms as *wit* and *sense* with an ultimate center of authority needs to be emphasized. The ultimate center and source of authority in this system of symbols is God, the prime mover and unitary source of value, the heavenly King; all other monarchs and authorities are no more than emblems of and derivations from the center of value. The chain is unbroken from the heavenly King to the earthly king and on to the poet. The connection of the poet and of wit and sense with ultimate authority is not enforced by weight of tradition to the extent that the earthly monarch's connection with the divine is, but there are enough conventional connections between the poet and authority that the prologues can create the poet monarch of his realm and can suggest the connection of terms like *wit* and *sense* with ultimate value by making them parts of the monarchal sequence.

A consideration of the themes with which the satiric stage poems as distinguished from the laudatory are occupied will exhibit a variety of disvalue symbols, and the various ways in which such symbols can be created. In these contexts, where the imagery is primarily engaged in disvaluing, established values and value symbols are still important because they usually appear, though briefly and sometimes muffled, to provide a point of reference. Among the pieces spoken in London, the lashing, satiric kind is very prominent.

In London are delivered the assaults upon the disorders that afflict poetry and criticism, the attacks on poetasters, on false critics, on fickle and presuming audiences. Bad poets are, first of all, those who are not makers; they deal in appearances and have no direct grasp of reality. They are imitators, copying the exterior features of plays and having, themselves, no direct contact with essences and the true act of making. The bad poet does not imitate nature by repeating in strict analogy the process of creation; the bad poet makes copies of copies. He is a composer dealing entirely in appearances and the external aspects of a drama:

> I'll write a Play, says one, for I have got
> A broad-brim'd hat, and wastbelt tow'rds a Plot.
> Sayes t'other, I have one more large than that:
> Thus they out-write each other with a hat.
> The brims still grew with every Play they writ;
> And grew so large, they cover'd all the wit.
> Hat was the Play: 'twas language, wit and tale:
> Like them that find, Meat, drink, and cloth, in Ale.
> What dulness do these Mungrill-wits confess
> When all their hope is acting of a dress!
>
> (P, *Conquest of Granada* I, ll. 9-18; I, 128K)

Here *wit* is the value term, the monarch, covered and all but obscured. Surrounding the value term is a cluster of metaphors for aesthetic disvalue—*a broad-brim'd hat, wastbelt, dress.* These are nontraditional metaphors arising out of the contemporary, though not really special, circumstance that a play had gained a resounding popular success by the appearance of Nokes, a famous comic actor, in outlandish dress as a caricature of the French fashion; some playwrights had then sought to repeat the success by outdoing the extremity of the original dress. Contemporary circumstances, not tradition, had laid the basis for the metaphor of aesthetic disvalue—*Hat was the Play*—and for the statement of the displacement of a legitimate value by a false value—*Hat was . . . wit.* The term *wit* holds its value position in these poems partly by agreement, *semper et ubique,* and additionally by the general and traditional analogies which have been applied to fortify it. Disvalue is also communicated, however, by attaching to the value term, *wit,* a forceful and unmistakable metaphor of the illegitimate, so that the combination *Mungrill-wits* designates false wit differently but as surely as *hat.* Disvalue is further communicated by pressing the *hat* metaphor up against

31

the wall of the absurd and impossible: *Thus they out-write each other with a hat.* The preposterousness of trying to write with a *hat* mirrors the preposterousness of taking the *hat* and *dress* for *wit.*

The bad poet, the poetaster, operates at too great a distance from originals and from the original process of making; he is separated, cut off, setting forth vain works and producing monsters because he does not reproduce originals, does not master substance, does not, in fact, create anything:

> Most Modern Wits, such monstrous Fools have shown,
> They seem'd not of heav'ns making but their own.
> Those Nauseous Harlequins in Farce may pass,
> But there goes more to a substantial Ass!
> Something of man must be expos'd to View,
> That, Gallants, they may more resemble you.
>
> (E, *Man of Mode,* ll. 1-6; I, 154C; I, 158K)

Here the common joke of a fool of God's own making, a natural, is wittily employed to set apart *monstrous Fools* as detached from nature. The joke is pursued even to the broadness of *substantial Ass,* but the special wit of the passage lies in the retention, without spoiling the joke, of a serious discrimination between a false making and a true making, between an *Entstehung aus nichts* and without valid form that does not imitate *heav'ns making,* and the substantial kind of creation where the poet is, like God, a maker.

The poetaster who is not a maker, who does not reproduce originals, has no center of authority to which his work refers. He is himself a slave to appearances and in no position to denounce his audience for being in the same bondage. He refers to no authority, no true oracle, no voice; he merely looks at his own reflection, the dumb image in the mirror:

> The thread-bare Author hates the gawdy Coat;
> And swears at the Guilt Coach, but swears a foot:
> For 'tis observ'd of every Scribling Man,
> He grows a Fop as fast as e'er he can;
> Prunes up, and asks his Oracle the Glass,
> If Pink or Purple best become his face.
>
> (E, *All For Love,* ll. 9-14; I, 165K)

Here there is a smothering atmosphere of appearances, the *Guilt*

Coach, the *gawdy Coat,* the absorbed attention to *face* and what becomes it, and value has all but left the scene. The author, who should appear as the agent of value, opposed to these mere surface values, is discovered first as envious and then as emulative of these surface values. It is only in the irony of *his Oracle the Glass* that value penetrates the context. *Oracle,* a voice pronouncing a divinely given word, jangles with and judges the context. It will by no means consort, except ironically, with the glass that dumbly renders back the face of the beholder. In place of analogy between realms there is here an oppugnance of realms, and the imagery acts to evaluate not by affiliation but by contrast.

The bad critic is related to the bad poet. If the good poet is both maker and knower, the good critic is both judge and knower; the best critic is himself a poet, a maker, so that his knowledge proceeds from and is directly of making, and his judgment accordingly is fortified by the direct knowledge of making. The bad critics, neither makers nor knowers, are, accordingly, stigmatized as usurpers, false authorities; the disvalue image involves the familiar transfer from the political to the aesthetic realm:

> From these Usurpers we appeal to you,
> The only knowing, only judging few.
>
> (P, *Circe,* ll. 29-30; I, 157C; I, 160K)

Some of the force of *Usurpers* as a disvalue image arises, of course, from the antithesis with the usual polar value image of monarch.

These false critics are poseurs; they have only the appearance of judges:

> But you, loud Sirs, who thro' your Curls look big,
> Criticks in Plume and white vallancy Wig,
> Who lolling on our foremost Benches sit,
> And still charge first, (the true forlorn of Wit)
> Whose favours, like the Sun, warm where you roul,
> Yet you like him, have neither heat nor Soul;
> So may your Hats your Foretops never press,
> Untouch'd your Ribbonds, sacred be your dress;
> So may you slowly to Old Age advance,
> And have th' excuse of Youth for Ignorance.
>
> (E, *Opening the New House,* ll.7-16; I, 150C; I, 379K)

33

Heav'n help the Man who for that face must drudge,
Which only has the wrinkles of a Judge.
(E, *All For Love*, ll. 26-27; I, 166K)

The false critics are attacked as loud, pompous, assertive, *forlorn of
Wit*, ironically exposed and rushed to their destruction by folly rather
than heroism. The wit which they have forsaken and which has
abandoned them is continuously active in Dryden's lines denouncing
critics who are totally lacking in the true fire and spirit, ignorant,
seeking to impose appearances as authority; these critics are all face,
surface, dress, hollow men having nothing within, no reality behind
their appearances, no authority behind their pretensions. They represent the transfer of values to appearances, the sanctification of dress,
and the clash of serious with trivial values is emphasized by an ironic
elevation of tone and style. The reverential tone, the mock prayer that
the *hat* may not disarrange the wig, that *Ribbonds* and *dress* may
have an untouchable sanctity, betrays these surfaces by the touch of
reverence, and reveals them for what they are. The combinations of
untouch'd and *Ribbonds, sacred* and *dress,* constitute the real disarray beneath the surface disarray which the prayer ostensibly seeks
to ward off. The situation of critics who have abandoned wit and
have been abandoned by wit suggests the absence of that monarch;
in the second passage, the value term *Judge* is betrayed by the surface, pseudo gravity of *wrinkles.*

As Dryden was fond of remarking in his essays, bad critics are
often simply metamorphosed bad writers. One of the prologues describes this development:

They who write Ill, and they who ne'r durst write,
Turn Critiques, out of meer Revenge and Spight:
A *Play-house* gives 'em Fame; and up there starts,
From a mean Fifth-rate Wit, a Man of Parts.
(So Common Faces on the Stage appear:
We take 'em in; and they turn Beauties here.)
Our Authour fears those Critiques as his Fate.
(P, *Conquest of Granada* II, ll. 1-7; I, 133K)

Wit is the value term which the absence of the monarch and the
presence of mere pretense devalue in *Fifth-rate.*

In the area of manners Dryden attacks extravagant behavior
of all sorts, addiction to change for the sake of change, blind pursuit

of the round of fashion, dull walking on the treadmill of fads. In the area of morals he stigmatizes vice generally, and especially vice as associated with hypocrisy. Deliberate incongruities between surface and interior, between face and virtue, fall under his most lashing criticism. The criticism of manners and morals focusses, sometimes with a fine irony, on unprincipled change as central and pervasive both in follies and vices:

> 'Twere well your Judgments but in Plays did range,
> But ev'n your Follies and Debauches change
> With such a Whirl, the Poets of your age
> Are tyr'd, and cannot score 'em on the Stage.
>
> .   .   .   .
>
> Our Fathers did for change to *France* repair,
> And they for change will try our *English* Air.
> As Children, when they throw one Toy away,
> Strait a more foolish Gugaw comes in play:
> So we, grown penitent, on serious thinking,
> Leave Whoring, and devoutly fall to Drinking.
> Scowring the Watch grows out of fashion wit
> Now we set up for Tilting in the Pit.
>
> (P, *Spanish Fryar*, ll.16-19, 33-40; I, 206-07K)

Here in the *whirl* of *change* there is a fine wit in the change that is rung upon the word itself (see the use of *change* in the sixth line above). *Whirl* is the image that rules here. *Whirl* is king, and in his topsy-turvy realm penitence and devotion can appear only ironically, relegated to governing a mere change and choice of vice between whoring and drinking. Wit, elsewhere imaged as a monarch, appears in this inverted realm subjected to the illegitimate government of mere fashion.

In the diary of the Royalist John Evelyn, with its record of the turmoil of the century—deposition and execution of the king, revolution, Commonwealth with no king, protectorate of Cromwell, restoration of Charles II, and the ensuing bitter conflict of Parliament and king, Whig and Tory, Church of England and Catholics, Church of England and dissenting sects—abhorrence of change and a fervent desire for a settled and stable order appear as a major theme, a Royalist *leitmotiv* that probably had a strong general appeal. Evelyn, of course, sees the Commonwealth men and Whigs as the agents of change; here is part of his entry for January 30, 1661: "This day (ô the stupendious, & inscrutable Judgements of God) were the Carkasses of that arch-rebell *Cromewell, Bradshaw* the Judge who condemn'd his Majestie & *Ireton,* sonn in law to the Usurper, draged out of their superbe Tombs (in Westminster among the Kings), to *Tyburne,* & hanged on the Gallows there from 9 in the morning til 6 at night, & then buried under that fatal & ignominious Monument, in a deepe pitt: Thousands of people (who had seene them in all their pride & pompous insults) being spectators: looke back at November 22: 1658 [the day of Cromwell's solemn and ceremonious funeral], & be astonish'd—*And fear God, & honor the King, but meddle not with them who are given to change.*"[10]

The urgently felt and expressed need for stability had, besides its historical occasion, an impressive literary ancestry. Not all times are equally turbulent, but instability and transience are literary themes in all periods; the instabilities of any historical era are, to the literary artist, symptoms of the deeper instabilities of human life. Boethius, searching out stability amid the welter of circumstances, provided Chaucer with the material for Theseus' confrontation, in *The Knight's Tale,* of the perennial problem, the sudden, shattering hammer blows of fortune, the bewildering shifts of circumstances, and, countering these, the philosophical organization of variety, discovering order, and the act of faith recognizing, affirming, and praising a divine order grounded on the great central stability of God. The theme appears in Spenser's *Mutability Cantos* where Mutability, a Titaness, challenges the rule of Jove, and marshals as evidence a crowded pageant of change, a pageant so inclusive and convincing that Nature's verdict against Mutability's plea seems frail, and the poet himself, shaken by the force of Mutability's argument, counters with a fervent prayer that he may be granted sight of an ultimate, unshaken order:

> For, all that moueth doth, in *change* delight:
> But thence-forth all shall rest eternally
> With Him that is the God of Sabbaoth hight:
> O that great Sabbaoth God, graunt me that Sabaoths sight.[11]

Order and hierarchy are a major theme of Shakespeare's plays, together with the shocked perception of the discord and disease which attack man and society when the order is broken.

The traditional theme is continued in Dryden's prologues and epilogues, and the medieval metaphor, so familiar in Shakespeare, is retained; change is repeatedly referred to as a disease, or as humoring the disease, of the body of society:

> Wee bring you change, to humour your Disease;
> Change for the worse has ever us'd to please.
>
> (P, *Albion and Albanius,* ll. 30-31; I, 457K)

The attack upon disorder in politics is directed against the Whigs, and against the effort to make the central authority of the ruler dependent upon the votes of majorities. All the terms which belong to the "state" (i.e., the republican form of government) as an entity different in kind from a monarchy are employed as terms of disvalue. The prologues attack Whigs, states, commonwealth, and votes as all involved on the side of quantity against quality, all involved in the dissipation of central authority; reformation and revolution are denounced, of course, as the extreme forms of the threat to a stable central authority:

> We grant an O'regrown Whig no grace can mend;
> But most are Babes, that know not they offend.
> The Crowd, to restless motion still enclin'd,
> Are Clouds, that rack according to the Wind.
>
> (P, *H.R.H. Return from Scotland,* ll. 30-33; I, 262-63K)

> Well Monarchys may own Religions name,
> But States are Atheists in their very frame.
>
> (P, *Amboyna,* ll. 21-22; I, 151K)

> Cry Freedom up with Popular noisy Votes:
> And get enough to cut each others Throats.
>
> .   .   .   .
>
> Doe, what in Coffee-houses you began;
> Pull down the Master, and Set up the Man.
>
> (P, *Duke of Guise,* ll. 30-31, 46-47; I, 327K)

Finally, this general satirical assault is carried on in the area of religion. The objects of the attack here are the Presbyterians and all the dissenting sects. They are attacked for their fanaticism, for setting up the private spirit against tradition, for trying to break the continuity which the established church traces back to the founder of the church; their members are assailed for pretensions and excesses of

37

zeal, for canting speech coupled with mercenary behavior, and for lack of true loyalty to the king. Some examples of these attacks follow:

> What if some one inspir'd with Zeal, shou'd call,
> Come let's go cry, God save him at *White-Hall?*
> His best friends wou'd not like this over-care:
> Or think him e're the safer for that pray'r.
> Five Praying Saints are by an Act allow'd:
> But not the whole Church-Militant, in crowd.
> Yet, should heav'n all the true Petitions drain ⎫
> Of *Presbyterians,* who wou'd Kings maintain; ⎬
> Of Forty thousand, five wou'd scarce remain. ⎭
>
> (P, *Loyal Brother,* ll. 46-54; I, 247-48K)

> Since Faction ebbs, and Rogues grow out of Fashion,
> Their penny-Scribes take care t' inform the Nation,
> How well men thrive in this or that Plantation.

> How *Pensilvania's* Air agrees with Quakers,
> And *Carolina's* with Associators:
> Both e'en too good for Madmen and for Traitors.

> Truth is, our Land with Saints is so run o'er,
> And every Age produces such a store,
> That now there's need of two *New-Englands* more.
>
> (P, *To King and Queen,* ll. 1-9; I, 323K)

Dryden's arguments are steadily centered on the question of authority. He regarded diffusion of authority in religion as inherently uncongenial to monarchy in secular government because he saw the monarch as the symbolic juncture of sacred and secular power. Dryden thought, like Hobbes, that for the sake of social order the private citizen's secular and religious decisions must recognize the monarchal authority. Otherwise religion and government were, in Dryden's view, subject to a splintering process at the hands of many monarchs—as many monarchs as consciences—and he could not envision, in such a situation, any feasible limits or control. The vigor and intensity of Dryden's language are aimed particularly at the pretense of loyalty to the king on the part of Presbyterians and dissenters because he thought that, given their religious ideas, their loyalty to the king *could* be no more than pretense. The true sentence for such views, fairly written by authority, and the true signature of such views, written by those who held them, were banishment and exile.

Another important method of valuation by means of imagery is the use of classical allusion. This method is closely akin to the valuation by affiliation and contrast between realms, aesthetic and political, aesthetic and religious, political and religious, but with the difference that the classical allusion is the gateway to one large realm which includes these other realms as provinces. Accordingly, though the transit may not be from the aesthetic realm to the religious realm, but simply from the English aesthetic realm to the classical aesthetic realm, the boundary that is crossed between English and classical has a significance for affiliation or for contrast that is comparable to the significance of crossing from the aesthetic to the religious realm, because the classical territory has been elevated by the veneration of centuries to something very close to a religious position, a value realm above history in which figures ranging from the gods through the godlike personages of epic to actual historical persons—Jove and Pallas, Aeneas and Hector, Caesar and Brutus—have a status, as images, approaching that of biblical figures—God, Christ, and Moses, David and Achitophel. It is in the prologues and epilogues to the University of Oxford that classical allusions appear in considerable numbers; they are usual features of the poems of compliment:

> What *Greece,* when Learning flourish'd, onely Knew,
> (*Athenian* Judges,) you this day Renew.
> Here too are Annual Rites to *Pallas* done,
> And here Poetique prizes lost or won.
> Methinks I see you, Crown'd with Olives sit,
> And strike a sacred Horrour from the Pit.
>
> (P, *Oxford, 1673,* ll. 1-6; I, 146C; I, 369K)

In this example the transit from the English to the classical realm is affiliative and appreciative; there is a transfusion of value from Greek to Oxonian learning, from Athenian to Oxonian aesthetic judgment, and it is particularly easy to see, in this case, that the transfer can be closely akin to an importation from the religious to the aesthetic realm because the comparisons touch upon the Greek deification of wisdom, and the Greek combination of aesthetic performance with religious ritual. The analogies are honorific, and the terms in which they transpire—*Annual Rites to Pallas; Crown'd with Olives; strike a sacred Horrour*—make the classical compliments akin to sanctification.

There are many illustrations of the appreciative kind of valuation in which the allusion is to the classical deities:

None of our living Poets dare appear,
For Muses so severe are worshipt here;
That conscious of their Faults they shun the Eye,
And as Prophane, from Sacred places fly,
Rather than see th' offended God, and dye.

. . . .

But when to Praise from you they would Aspire
Though they like Eagles Mount, your *Jove* is Higher.
(P, *Oxford, 1674*, ll. 23-27, 36-37; I, 152C; I, 372-73K)

The first instance above is interesting because it offers another kind of evidence that allusions to the classical deities can import religious value akin to the sanctification invoked by allusions to the Christian deity and biblical figures. From the metaphor of Oxford as a shrine for the worship of severe muses the verse slips easily and directly into an image of Oxford as the seat of the Old Testament God; the final triplet is based on the representation of God in Exodus 33:20: "And he said, Thou canst not see my face: for there shall no man see me, and live."

Oxford is affiliated not only with the classical deities that preside over learning and the arts and with the classical religious and aesthetic rites, but also with social aspects of the antique world:

His [Bathurst's] Learning, and untainted Manners too
We find (*Athenians*) are deriv'd to you;
Such Ancient hospitality there rests
In yours, as dwelt in the first *Grecian* Breasts,
Whose kindness was Religion to their Guests.
Such Modesty did to our sex appear,
As had there been no Laws we need not fear,
Since each of you was our Protector here.
Converse so chast, and so strict Vertue shown,
As might *Apollo* with the Muses own.
(E, *Oxford, 1674*, ll. 21-30; I, 153C; I, 373-74K)

40

Even at the level of compliment to manners, however, the Grecian comparisons are not left to transfer value simply from ancient and honorable custom to modern Oxonian behavior; the compliment is enhanced by further reference to the religious basis of hospitality in the antique world. The analogy is made strong by importing both the cultural fact and the religious ideal that lay behind it. The compliment is given its final elevation by the comparison of Oxonian conversation and behavior to those of Apollo with the Muses. The transfer of value here is twice enhanced so that the total accession to Oxford includes something like the epic range from the behavior of men founded upon an ideal (e.g., Alcinous' hospitable entertainment of Odysseus) to that ideal behavior in an ideal embodiment among the gods.

Political institutions of the ancient world are also alluded to in the compliments to Oxford:

> But by the Sacred Genius of this Place,
> By every Muse, by each Domestick Grace,
> Be kind to Wit, which but endeavours well,
> And, where you judge, presumes not to excel.
> Our Poets hither for Adoption come,
> As Nations su'd to be made Free of *Rome;*
> Not in the suffragating Tribes to stand,
> But in your utmost, last, Provincial Band.
> If His Ambition may those Hopes pursue,
> Who with Religion loves Your Arts and You,
> *Oxford* to Him a dearer Name shall be,
> Than His own Mother University.
> *Thebes* did His Green, unknowing Youth ingage,
> He chuses *Athens* in His Riper Age.
>   (P, *Oxford, 1676,* ll. 25-38; I, 156C; I, 375-76K)

The compliment here is of special interest because the transfer of value is primarily from the classical political realm to the modern aesthetic realm, Oxford's position in relation to poets being compared to Rome's position in relation to nations seeking free provincial status in the empire. The primary consideration here is the tenor of a widely respected authority, as in the affiliation of aesthetic and political realms involved in comparing poets to monarchs. Yet the political realm should not be dismissed altogether because Oxford is, among other things, a stronghold of the royalist cause, an actual and symbolic center of the king's power; it was the scene of one of Charles II's greatest political successes, the demonstration of royalist strength which culminated in the dissolution of the Oxford Parliament on March 28, 1681, and the scurrying flight of the Whig members from the town. This fact about Oxford appears plainly in a prologue to Oxford apparently written shortly after that event:

> When *London* Votes with *Southwark's* disagree,
> Here they may find their long lost Loyalty.
> Here busie Senates, to th' old Cause inclin'd,
> May snuff the Votes their Fellows left behind.
>
> (P, *Oxford, 1681*, ll. 11-14; II, 841K)

Even in the poems of compliment, however, the classical allusions have other uses besides the honorific; the concluding couplet of the first passage above provides an instance:

> *Thebes* did His Green, unknowing Youth ingage,
> He chuses *Athens* in His Riper Age.

This contrasted set of metaphors, Thebes for Cambridge and Athens for Oxford, shows the use of classical allusion to limit and negate as well as to extend. Thebes was subdued by Athens in Theseus' legendary unification of Greece; Athens was the ultimate center of an order, Thebes the last major rebel. Athens was remarkable for the combination of strength and wisdom (Pallas Athena, its patron goddess, the patroness of the liberal arts conventionally represented in armed guise), Thebes for energies issuing in discord and sudden violences (such as Creon's) and reflecting its foundation by the sowing of the Martian teeth; Thebes also had a reputation for dullness. Thebes is the choice of *Green, unknowing Youth,* Athens the choice of knowing *Riper Age.*

There are occasions, too, in these poems of compliment when classical allusion is employed still more unmitigatedly as a means of depreciating and disvaluing. For example:

> So Poetry, which is in *Oxford* made
> An Art, in *London* onely is a Trade.
> There Haughty Dunces whose unlearned Pen
> Could ne'er Spell Grammar, would be reading Men.
> Such build their Poems the *Lucretian* way,

42

So many Huddled Atoms make a Play,
And if they hit in Order by some Chance,
They call that Nature, which is Ignorance.

(P, Oxford, 1673, ll. 28-35; I, 146-47C; I, 370K)

The atomistic theory of Lucretius in his *De Rerum Natura* as a metaphor for the unrelated parts of aesthetically poor works is an interesting case of the definitive and disvaluative use of classical allusion, although in this case the transition from philosophy to aesthetic practice is not an even movement from disvalue in one realm to disvalue in another. *Lucretian* by itself is not enough to do the damage; *So many Huddled Atoms* and *hit in Order by some Chance* are necessary to supply a depreciative content to *Lucretian* for the disvaluing of poems and plays. The philosophy of Lucretius is not assailed. The imagery acts against bad poems and plays, but Lucretius as philosopher remains neutral and receives only accidental damage. As belonging to the classical realm, Lucretius continues to possess here a certain stable honor, for he is referred to by a learned pen and is a part of that pen's distinction from the *unlearned Pen* that is here being assailed; Lucretius is also honored by the assumption that at Oxford, where poetry is an art and where learning flourishes, it is proper to allude to him.

A few lines farther along in the same prologue classical allusion is used again to diminish and disvalue:

Our Poet, could he find Forgiveness here
Would wish it rather than a *Plaudit* there [in London].
He owns no Crown from those *Praetorian* bands,
But knows *that* Right is in this Senates hands.

(P, Oxford, 1673, ll. 38-41; I, 147C; I, 370K)

The Praetorian guards and their forceful intervention in the choice of Roman emperors are here disvalued by contrast with the legal election of emperors by the Roman senate. The value and disvalue transfers occur between the political and the aesthetic realm, and the tenor of the transaction is authority; as in the previous case, the *political* nature of the authority conferred upon Oxford is incidental, but, in view of Oxford's political status, not irrelevant. In the disvalue transfer, it is perhaps even more obvious that although the metaphor disvalues the aesthetic judgment of London audiences, the *political* nature of the metaphor also disvalues the *vox populi* of the London

43

Whigs as incompetent to bestow or withhold the crown from a legiti-mate monarch. Beside *Senate, Praetorian bands* is depreciative, as Thebes beside Athens, but there is a difference between this kind of depreciation and the abusive phrases of the London prologues such as *damned Whigs*. Disvaluation, by classical allusion or by other means, is infrequent in the Oxford prologues, which are mainly occupied with compliment and praise, but the pole of value, so powerful here and so often attended by classical metaphors, commands a decorum which extends to the opposite pole and dictates a more than ordinary moderation in the expression of disvalue in order that the dominant tone of dignity and veneration may not be disrupted. The classical metaphors, by translating both value and disvalue from the dust and heat of the contemporary arena, preserve and define, distance with-out destroying, the conflict between them. The classical analogies are like other analogies in being evaluative, but as they are more remote, belonging to a formed and finished world, they are more judicious as images, more authoritative in their judgment. The only com-parably authoritative matrix of evaluative imagery is the Bible.

The full effect of any image may be conditioned to a significant extent by the presence of another image. Such conditioning, in an obvious form, has been touched upon in cases of antithesis. In such cases the effect of one image upon another is thrust upon the reader by their close juxtaposition and syntactical connection. Relations be-tween images have also appeared in the discussion of the repetition of a given image in various poems and with various tenors; this kind of relationship among images has the effect of suggesting a basic uni-formity of theme, or the linear connection of one theme with another. There are also cases, however, in which images occurring within a single poem and not necessarily standing in any close syntactical relationship interact and affect one another, and cases in which a sequence or chain of images within a poem is significant. An ex-ample of the former sort appears in the following prologue; the first group of lines is the beginning of the prologue, the second group the end:

> What Flocks of Critiques hover here to day,
> As Vultures wait on Armies for their Prey,
> All gaping for the Carcass of a Play!

With Croaking Notes they bode some dire event;
And follow dying Poets by the scent.
Ours gives himself for gone; y'have watch'd your time!
He fights this day unarm'd; without his Rhyme.

.　　.　　.　　.　　.　　.　　.　　.　　.

But, as the Rich, when tir'd with daily Feasts,
For change, become their next poor Tenants Ghests;
Drink hearty Draughts of Ale, from plain brown Bowls,
And snatch the homely Rasher from the Coals:
So you, retiring from much better Cheer,
For once, may venture to do penance here.
And since that plenteous Autumn now is past,
Whose Grapes and Peaches have Indulg'd your taste,
Take in good part from our poor Poets boord,
Such rivell'd Fruits as Winter can afford.

(P, All For Love, ll. 1-7, 31-40; I, 164-65K)

The initial images deal with the relationship of the poet to the critics,
the final comparisons with the relationship of the poet to fellow poets.
In the first passage the imagery places the poet in a perilous but
honorable situation; he is a despairing, unarmed warrior. The vulture
image for the critics is a good example of a *semper et ubique* disvalue
image, the reduction of human status by comparison to a generally
loathed creature. The poet represents himself and his play as in peril
of death and of being devoured by the carrion-eating vultures who
gape *for the Carcass of a Play.* The feast that is toward in Death's
eternal cell is a very grim repast.

In the second passage, however, the imagery creates the picture
of an altogether different meal. The poet appears as a more modest,
less endangered figure, the poor tenant entertaining the rich land-
owner; if his status is humble, he has still the honor of being the host.
The glowing fire and *hearty Draughts of Ale* vividly create the atmosphere of homely good cheer. The homeliness of the meal provided by the poet is steadily stressed, most emphatically in the *rivell'd
Fruits* of the last line; nevertheless, the poet is represented as hos-
pitably offering what his lean larder affords, and pressing for a gracious and good-humored acceptance of his invitation. There is even
the suggestion, in *penance,* of the religious virtue of simplicity.

The images of the initial and final passages, of course, clearly
affect each other as contrast. There is, for the poet, all the difference

45

of Hamlet's distinction, "not where he eats but where he is eaten," or, more accurately, all the difference between being and providing the meal. There is also the distinction between a vicious tearing of flesh and a meal in a warm human atmosphere, governed by social decorum, hospitable, even ceremonious. Aside from the clear contrasts of the images, however, there is the matter of their sequence. The effect of sequence, in this case, is to suggest the poet's movement from an atmosphere of hostility to one of acceptance, from a situation of brave peril to one of humble security. The movement from the initial to the final images, however, is not altogether an implied movement arising simply from the statement of the two positions. There are several intervening points where the imagery suggests the movement of transition:

> A brave Man scorns to quarrel once a day;
> Like Hectors, in at every petty fray.
>
> .   .   .   .
>
> Fops may have leave to level all they can;
> As Pigmies wou'd be glad to lopp a Man.
> Half-Wits are Fleas; so little and so light;
> We scarce cou'd know they live, but that they bite.
>
> (P, *All For Love*, ll. 21-22, 27-30; I, 164-65K)

The initial situation of the unarmed warrior facing a grim and apparently ineluctable fate is left behind by the image of the brave warrior, controlling his fate, able to choose not to enter a petty fray. In the second passage even this position is left behind and the very possibility of a quarrel disappears with the deterioration of the opposition; the first passage had a petty, but still a human conflict, but the imagery of the second passage moves on down to *Pigmies* and then to *Fleas*. All peril has disappeared; there remains only annoyance. The poet simply as man is superior to these trivia; the imagery has moved from the tearing beaks of vultures to the bite of a flea. The imagery of the poet as warrior has gradually faded out, and the poem glides directly into its final extended image of the poet as the poor tenant and humble host. The contrast between the initial and final images of a meal implies the movement of the poet from one position to another; intervening images fill in some stages of that movement. There is, in other words, a kind of action in the imagery, and the major contrasting images are the termini of that action.

We have seen, in these prologues and epilogues, that imagery plays an important rôle in evaluating the contemporary scene. The social, political, aesthetic, and religious facts of the day are drawn into analogies; an interpretation is put upon the facts. Description of this evaluative process in the imagery of these poems is not complete until one has surveyed the final effects of multiple analogy upon a key value image such as *monarch,* and the effects of clusters of value images upon one general tenor, such as *Oxford.* The description of these effects leads to the definition of a special kind of metaphor.

In the case of the monarch image we have seen that it appears in a broad range of analogic positions, and that for terms such as wit, sense, and beauty, for figures such as poets, for an institution such as Oxford, the image is a stamp of authority and a hallmark of value. We have also remarked that the authority of the image is partially derived from the conventional affiliation of the monarch with God; this affiliation appears clearly in passages where the political monarch is the tenor of the discussion:

> Our Royal Master will'd it should be so,
> What e're He's pleas'd to own, can need no show:
> That Sacred Name gives Ornament and Grace.
> (P, *Opening the New House,* ll.30-32; I, 149C; I, 378K)

The political-religious affiliation appears also when the monarch is the vehicle of analogy:

> But *Shakespear's* pow'r is sacred as a King's.
> (P, *The Tempest,* l. 24; I, 117K)

Monarch is an image that ranges in application from the humbly secular to the most high and sanctified, and even in its humbler applications may trail clouds of its brightest glory. The affiliations of the monarch image, moreover, represent not the special ingenuities of poetic association, but the characteristic and habitual associations which existed most emphatically in the minds of the king's loyal supporters and to some extent in the minds of all Englishmen. Political events of the mid-seventeenth-century had provided the most powerful kind of contemporary impetus to the traditional sacred affiliation of the king; Hobbes, in his *Leviathan* (1651), gives the following example of an ordinary train of association: "This Trayne of Thoughts, or Mentall Discourse, is of two sorts. The first is *Un-*

guided, without Designe, and inconstant. . . . And yet in this wild ranging of the mind, a man may oft-times perceive the way of it, and the dependance of one thought upon another. For in a Discourse of our present civill warre, what could seem more impertinent, than to ask (as one did) what was the value of a Roman Penny? *Yet the Cohaerence to me was manifest enough* [italics mine]. For the Thought of the warre, introduced the Thought of the delivering up the King to his Enemies; The Thought of that, brought in the Thought of the delivering up of Christ; and that again the Thought of the 30 pence, which was the price of that treason: and thence easily followed that malicious question; and all this in a moment of time; for Thought is quick."[12] Here is an instance of the same sort of association in the metaphors of one of Dryden's prologues. Speaking of loyalty to the king:

> Let his own Servants turn, to save their stake;
> Glean from his plenty, and his wants forsake.
> But let some *Judas* near his Person stay,
> To swallow the last Sop, and then betray.
>
> (P, *Duke of Guise,* ll. 37-40; I, 327K)

The special impetus to this affiliation of the king with Christ had been provided by the execution of Charles I which, during the period of the Commonwealth, had assumed, in the minds of the royalists, the status of martyrdom. The martyrology of Charles I begins in earnest with the publication of *Eikon Basilike* (1649), the purported meditations of the imprisoned monarch; a volume entitled *Reliquiae Sacrae Carolinae. Or the Works of that Great Monarch and Glorious Martyr King Charles the I* was printed at The Hague in 1650; it contains the civil and sacred remains of Charles I, a main part of the latter being *Eikon Basilike.* Facing the title page there is an allegorical woodcut or emblem representing Charles I in confinement, his foot spurning the world below and the vanities of an earthly crown, his hand grasping a crown of thorns, and his gaze fixed upon heaven where there appears a blessed and eternal crown of glory.

It is important to realize that the martyrology of Charles I did not disappear with the Restoration but received a fresh emphasis. A special service was added to the liturgy for January 30, the day of Charles I's execution, and that date was kept as a day of fasting and humiliation. (The service appointed for use on this date was not removed from the prayer book until 1859.) In his preface to *Religio Laici* (1682) Dryden speaks of "the Reign of King *Charles* the Martyr." As late as 1685 John Evelyn records in his *Diary,* in the course of a discussion of miracles, the following instances: "To all which the Bishop added a greate Miracle happning in that Citty of Winchester to his certaine knowledge, of a poore miserably sick & decrepit Child, (as I remember long kept un-baptized) who immediately on his Baptisme, recover'd; as also of the sanatory effect of *K. Charles* his Majesties fathers blood, in healing one that was blind."[13] Charles I, who, even in Marvell's account, "nothing common did or mean/ Upon that memorable scene" of his execution, was affiliated more closely than his successors with the image of Christ and His sufferings, but his successors, Charles II and James II, maintained some of the traditional connection of the king with miraculous powers. The ceremony of the king touching for the evil continued through the reigns of Charles II and of James II; it is several times mentioned by Evelyn.

The continuation, after the Restoration, of the struggle for power between king and Parliament probably conditions two opposite features of the monarch image as it appears in the prologues and epilogues: the monarch as a sacred and powerful figure, and the monarch as a sacred and threatened, long-suffering, martyred figure. The distance between these aspects of the monarch image is the distance between the ideal monarch in his ideal condition and the ideal monarch in his actual condition, the distinction between God the almighty Father and God the suffering Son. These two resources of the monarch image are both useful in the value analogies. They provide the means for representing the nature of value and enacting the fate of value. Wit, like the monarch, is a value and should dwell in a palace; in the Oxford prologues one finds wit and the monarch enthroned and powerful. Wit, like the monarch, may be assailed and deposed; in the London prologues one finds rebellious turmoil against the monarch and the *anarchy of wit*. In other words, *monarch,* running the course of its various analogic positions, acquires a rich metaphoric content. It acquires a history from its political position, and from its religious position it acquires the sacred analogue of that history and its value; dramatists are *Like Monarchs, ruin'd with expensive war* playing *the Tragedy of Wit* (P, *Aureng-Zebe,* ll. 38-40;

49

I, 157K), or their power is *sacred as a King's* (P, *The Tempest*, 1. 24; I, 117K). Between obedience and rebellion, between enthronement and deposition the metaphor of the monarch moves back and forth, enacting on the one hand the *Tragedy of Wit*, the turning away from value; on the other the blessed hope of a return:

> What Civil Broils have cost we know too well,
> Oh let it be enough that once we fell,
> And every Heart conspire with every Tongue,
> Still to have such a King, and this King Long.
>
> (P, *Unhappy Favourite*, ll. 31-34; I, 245K)

The movement between the two positions of the monarch synchronizes with the movement from satire to praise. Moreover, rebellion and obedience, deposition and enthronement develop their own special metaphoric locations in the satiric and complimentary prologues and epilogues. London is one of these locations:

> Make *London* independant of the Crown:
> A Realm apart; the Kingdom of the Town.
> Let *Ignoramus* Juries find no Traitors:
> And *Ignoramus* Poets scribble Satyres.
>
> (P, *Duke of Guise*, ll. 41-44; I, 327K)

> 'Tis not our want of Wit that keeps us Poor,
> For then the Printers Press would suffer more:
> Their [Whig] Pamphleteers each day their Venom spit,
> They thrive by Treason and we starve by Wit.
>
> . . . .
>
> Such are the Authors who have run us down,
> And Exercis'd you Critticks of the Town.
>
> (E, *Unhappy Favourite*, ll. 16-19, 24-25; I, 245K)

> The Plays that take on our Corrupted Stage,
> Methinks resemble the distracted Age;
> Noise, Madness, all unreasonable Things,
> That strike at Sense, as Rebels do at Kings!
>
> . . . .
>
> They talk of Feavours that infect the Brains,
> But Non-sence is the new Disease that reigns.
>
> (P, *Loyal General*, ll. 12-15, 20-21; I, 163C; I, 205K)

London is represented as in rebellion against the king; there treason is thriving and not found out; wit is starving; noise and madness are striking, like rebels, against sense; the king's authority is being denied and illegitimate rulers are taking his place; nonsense, a disease, reigns. Analogies make the monarch who is here deposed a nexus of value. London is agent, and scene, of the deposition of value.

Oxford is the other location where the monarch and the values over which he presides are enthroned in strength. At Oxford wit does not starve, and treason does not thrive; here loyalty thrives, and there is forgiveness for the sins of the other place. Here the monarch flourishes and sends abroad poets to cultivate the virtue which he sows. Here the monarch may dwell in blessedness; the place has a sacred genius:

> *Oxford's* a place, where Wit can never sterve.
> > (P, *Oxford, 1680,* l. 36; I, 165C; I, 375K)
> The Wit we lost in Town, we find in you.
> Our Poets their fled Parts may draw from hence,
> And fill their windy Heads with sober Sense.
> > (P, *Oxford, 1681,* ll. 8-10; II, 841K)
> Our Poets hither for Adoption come.
> > (P, *Oxford, 1676,* l. 29; I, 156C; I, 376K)
> As your Commissioners our Poets goe,
> To Cultivate the Virtue which you sow:
> In your *Lycaeum,* first themselves refind,
> And Delegated thence to Humane kind.
> But as Embassadours, when long from home,
> For new Instructions to their Princes come;
> So Poets who your Precepts have forgot,
> Return, and beg they may be better taught.
>
> . . . .
>
> Our Poet, could he find Forgiveness here. . . .
> > (P, *Oxford, 1673,* ll. 12-19, 38; I, 146-47C; I, 369-70K)
> Here they may find their long lost Loyalty.
> > (P, *Oxford, 1681,* l. 12; II, 841K)
> Blest sure are you above all Mortal kind.
> > (P, *Oxford, 1674,* l. 15; I, 152C; I, 372K)
> But by the Sacred Genius of this Place. . . .
> > (P, *Oxford, 1676,* l. 25; I, 156C; I, 375K)

The apotheosis of value that occurs at Oxford is, of course, more than the actual university can prosaically bear. In one of his letters Dryden shows his awareness that such poetic treatment included flattery: "I have sent Your Lordship a prologue and epilogue which I made for our players when they went down to Oxford. I heare, since they have succeeded; And by the event your Lordship will judge how easy 'tis to passe any thing upon an University; and how grosse flattery the learned will endure."[14] There are two ways of taking these remarks: either Dryden, with an easy cynicism, is convicting himself of gross flattery of the learned and of Oxford, or he is indicating in the expression "passe any thing upon an University" that the true subject of these prologues and epilogues to the university is something beyond the university; then the learned who take themselves and the actual university as the objects of the praise that is in these poems would, indeed, be grossly flattering themselves. It is certainly possible that Dryden is pointing to a difference between the actual Oxford and Oxford in an ideal conception, between the university as it is in fact and the idea of a university, or between the university and what it can be made to stand for, what, as a symbol, it can bear. Yet if Dryden is pointing to the difference between the actual university and the idea of a university, he is also making use of the continuity or partial congruity between the particular local and historical fact and the universal value of which it is an imperfect embodiment; the congruity that keeps gross flattery in touch with propriety and makes it possible for the actual audience to appropriate the terms of the poetry to itself prevents the terms from becoming simply absurd.

This method of imaging is not without example. Donne's *Anniversaries,* for instance, were censured by Ben Jonson as gross flattery of a mortal woman, acceptable and proper only if they were understood to have for their real subject not Elizabeth Drury but the Virgin Mary, or an ideal center of value. The possibility of using Elizabeth Drury as a metaphor depends upon the establishment of some congruity or continuity between her and the value that is to be metaphorized, but Donne actually manages to make do with a relatively slight congruity. It is the nature of metaphor, of course, to speak of Elizabeth Drury as if she were the value center, and this situation appears generally in poems of compliment; the occasioning person is departed from and praised by way of an idealization, a metaphor.

Among the ultimate effects of the analogies in Dryden's prologues and epilogues, among the ultimate resources of their imagery, must be numbered the metaphoric action given to the *monarch* image and to the values associated with that image, as well as the metaphors created at the two extremes of that action, *London* for values deposed and fallen, and *Oxford* for values maintained on their throne.

NOTES

1. *Lives of the Poets,* ed. G. B. Hill (3 vols., Oxford, 1905), I, 367.

2. A number of editors and critics have recognized a literary difference between the London and Oxford pieces. Louis Bredvold observes: "A noticeably higher tone is evident in the prologues and epilogues which he composed especially for the visits of the players to Oxford"—*The Best of Dryden,* ed. Louis I. Bredvold (New York: The Ronald Press Co., 1933), p. 538. Ingo Rösecke, in his detailed study of them, discusses the London and the Oxford prologues and epilogues in separate groups, and comments on the basis for the distinction: "Zwischen den Londoner Bühnenpro- und -epilogen und den Oxfordern besteht auf den ersten Blick ein fundamentaler Unterschied. Mit ihrer einheitlichen Ausrichtung fallen die letzteren völlig aus dem Rahmen der bisher behandelten Vor- und Nachsprüche heraus. Selbst Drydens Zeitgenossen fiel die Wandlung in Sprache und—in beschränktem Masse—auch Inhalt bei den Pro- und Epilogen auf"—*Drydens Prologe und Epiloge* (Hamburg, 1938), p. 121. Dryden himself indicates the difference:

He, whose undaunted Muse, with Loyal Rage,
Has never spar'd the Vices of the Age,
Here finding nothing that his Spleen can raise,
Is forc'd to turn his Satire into Praise.
(P, Oxford, 1681, ll. 27-30; II, 841K)

3. *The Spectator,* ed. Henry Morley (London, 1891), No. 341, p. 497.

4. Dryden sometimes had the prologue and epilogue printed and circulated copies among his friends, but probably most members of the audience had to rely on hearing alone. This practice of Dryden's, however, is an interesting indication of the importance which he attached to these poems. Furthermore, it suggests that these pieces were designed to bear closer inspection, and that the reader might be rewarded with implications beyond those which the auditor could be expected to gather.

5. Samuel Holt Monk, "From Jacobean to Augustan," *Southern Review,* VII (1941-42), 366.

6. In this chapter the symbols "P" and "E" are introduced to identify, respectively, prologues and epilogues, and short titles or abbreviated descriptions have been used to identify some of the poems. The following list records the abbreviations used and the fuller title or description for which they stand in the cases that might present any difficulty:

H. R. H. Return from Scotland	*To His Royal Highness Upon His first appearance at the Duke's Theatre since his Return from Scotland*
Opening the New House	*Spoken at the Opening of the New House* (March 26, 1674)
Oxford, 1673	*To the University of Oxon.* [1673]
Oxford, 1674	*To the University of Oxford, 1674*
Oxford, 1676	*To the University of Oxford* [1676]
Oxford, 1680	*To the University of Oxford* [1680]
Oxford, 1681	*To the University of Oxford, 1681*
To King and Queen	*To the King and Queen at the Opening of Their Theatre*

7. Compare T. S. Eliot's symbolic expansion by way of "watermen"—*fishmen*—in *The Waste Land*, III, ll. 257-65.

8. See, for example, the Prologue to *The Unhappy Favourite*:

What Civil Broils have cost we know too well,
Oh let it be enough that once we fell.

(ll. 31-32; I, 245K)

9. The analogy, frequent in Dryden's poetry, is perhaps most familiar in *Absalom and Achitophel*:

The God-like *David* spoke: with awfull fear
His Train their Maker in their Master hear.

(ll. 937-38; I, 241K)

10. *The Diary of John Evelyn,* ed. E. S. de Beer (6 vols., Oxford, 1955), III, 269.

11. *The Faerie Queene* ("Two Cantos of Mutabilitie"), VII, 8, ii, in *The Poetical Works of Edmund Spenser,* ed. J. C. Smith and E. De Selincourt (Oxford, 1912), p. 406. All citations of Spenser are from this edition.

12. Thomas Hobbes, *Leviathan* (Oxford, 1909), pp. 19-20.

13. *The Diary,* IV, 469.

14. To John Wilmot, Earl of Rochester, in *The Letters of John Dryden,* ed. Charles E. Ward (Durham, N.C.: Duke University Press, 1942), p. 10.

III

A Layman's Faith

O TURN FROM Dryden's prologues and epilogues to his *Religio Laici* (1682) is to turn away from both satire and praise to a kind of poetry lying somewhere between them. The voice that speaks in the prologues and epilogues commands many tones and subtle variations of tone, but these tones and their variations are mainly between the reproachful and the lashing on the one hand, and on the other between the commendatory and the fervently encomiastic; one range is from *Praetorian bands* to *Damn'd Whiggs, Rogues, Traitors, Madmen* and the other range is from *Lawfull Monarchs* to monarchs like *Angels* and like *Heav'n,* to a place of a *Sacred Genius* and those *Blest . . . above all Mortal kind.* In these short pieces spoken from the stage, where the gestures of imagery toward value and disvalue must be swift, sure, and obvious, the imagery appeals to the passions of the audience by diminishing or magnifying its objects. In *Religio Laici* the frankly partisan voice from the stage is replaced by the *persona* of a reasonable man writing a letter to a friend. The moderate voice of this poem still has the range from reverent praise to a vigorous, spurning blame, but the extreme reaches are occasional departures from a characteristic middle tone. Generally neither railing nor soaring to an *O altitudo,* the discourse projects the image of the good man, modest, upright, fair-minded, judicious.

The territory occupied by this poem is defined by Dryden in his preface: "It remains that I acquaint the Reader, that the Verses were written for an ingenious young Gentleman my Friend; upon his Translation of *The Critical History of the Old Testa-*

ment, compos'd by the learned Father *Simon*: The Verses therefore are address'd to the Translatour of that Work, and the style of them is, what it ought to be, Epistolary.

"If any one be so lamentable a Critique as to require the Smoothness, the Numbers and the Turn of Heroick Poetry in this Poem; I must tell him, that if he has not read *Horace,* I have studied him, and hope the style of his Epistles is not ill imitated here. The Expressions of a Poem, design'd purely for Instruction, ought to be Plain and Natural, and yet Majestick: for here the Poet is presum'd to be a kind of Law-giver, and those three qualities which I have nam'd are proper to the Legislative style. The Florid, Elevated and Figurative way is for the Passions; for Love and Hatred, Fear and Anger, are begotten in the Soul by shewing their Objects out of their true proportion; either greater than the Life, or less; but Instruction is to be given by shewing them what they naturally are. A Man is to be cheated into Passion, but to be reason'd into Truth" (I, 310-11K).

In spite of Dryden's indication of a range between plainness and majesty, the opening of the poem has surprised some critics; Professor A. W. Verrall speaks of the poem's "astounding commencement" and remarks: "That this is a mere assumption for a political purpose, I cannot admit; after reading the Preface, the opening of the poem surprises me fresh every time."[1]* Something of the same surprise is probably latent in the special admiration which other critics have expressed for the opening lines; Walter Savage Landor is recorded as having said: "Nothing was ever written in hymn equal to the beginning of Dryden's *Religio Laici,*—the first eleven lines."[2]

The beginning of the poem is not so astonishing when one recognizes, as did Dr. Johnson for example, that a middle style is not all of a level, but has a range of expression that includes, on one side, "high poetry"; Dr. Johnson says of the poem: "This however is a composition of great excellence in its kind, in which the familiar is very properly diversified with the solemn, and the grave with the humorous; in which metre has neither weakened the force nor clouded the perspicuity of argument: nor will it be easy to find another example equally happy of this middle kind of writing, which, though

Notes for this chapter are on page 71.

prosaick in some parts, rises to high poetry in others, and neither towers to the skies nor creeps along the ground."[3]

Dryden chose to rise swiftly to a height at the very beginning. It is instructive to remember, as one confronts the first eleven lines, that they are one of the passages that survived in the general wreck of Dryden's reputation in the nineteenth century when so many other examples of his middle style were consigned to a prose museum:

> Dim, as the borrow'd beams of Moon and Stars
> To *lonely, weary, wandring* Travellers,
> Is *Reason* to the *Soul*: And as on high,
> Those rowling Fires *discover* but the Sky
> Not light us *here;* So *Reason's* glimmering Ray ⎫
> Was lent, not to *assure* our *doubtfull* way, ⎬
> But *guide* us upward to a *better Day.* ⎭
> And as those nightly Tapers disappear
> When Day's bright Lord ascends our Hemisphere;
> So pale grows *Reason* at *Religions* sight;
> So *dyes,* and so *dissolves* in *Supernatural Light.*
>
> (ll. 1-11; I, 311K)

These lines are the plain and natural drawn up in their most majestic assemblage. The logic of this "surprise" may be founded upon the following considerations. (1) A discursive poem, in the absence of a fable, does not have a climax assigned by the fable where style and imagery must achieve their most notable elevation. (2) The two moments of a discourse that are naturally special and therefore most readily presented in special form are the beginning and the end, as is the case, for example, with the formalities that begin and end a letter. (3) In argument, the mobilization of unusual force in the middle or at the end is perilous because it may then appear as ancillary to objection, or as the belated storming of a position that has theretofore resisted the assault of argument; in both cases the mobilization of unusual force signalizes unusual strength in the opposition. (4) One object of the "surprise" opening is to secure a position that can be held throughout the argument; withdrawals at any minor points appear then as the concessions of strength, not the necessities of weakness.

Since a strong beginning at the wrong place could be a fatally wasted motion, the nature of the position initially assumed in this poem needs to be examined. The examination, to be complete, must include a study of how the position is taken up, and, finally, of course, why this particular position is chosen. What is to be said about the management of the imagery of this poem as an aspect of the middle style described by Dr. Johnson will appear when the imagery of the opening passage has been examined in some detail and considered in relation to the imagery of the rest of the poem.

One of the strongest emphases that verse can manage announces a position at the beginning of the poem. *Dim,* first word, first line, the crucial, qualifying predicate adjective, dislocated and emphasized by the syntactical inversion which suspends copula and subject, must be held like a very long note until the third line begins with *Is Reason to the Soul.* The simile which is interposed to create the suspension is clearly involved in the strategy of statement; the position of the simile emphasizes the predicate *Dim* by delaying the completion of the sense, and by delaying that completion just long enough so that copula and subject are thrust into an emphatic position at the beginning of the third line. One side of the position is firmly drawn by this powerful assertion of the dimness of Reason to the soul.[4] The other side of the position is established by the cumulative assertion of brightness, first brighter than Reason, then bright as day, then bright as the sun, then supernaturally bright; it is only near the end of the sequence (1. 10) that the tenor of the growing brightness is announced as Religion. Matter and manner cooperate to state both sides of the position, Reason and Religion, as well as the relation between these tenors, by identifying both with light and pressing Reason toward the lower and Religion to the upper limit on the scale of degree of brightness.

The extension and elaboration of the opening comparisons actually state in compressed form an extraordinary amount of what is to be said and demonstrated in the whole course of the argument about the relations of Reason and Religion. The figures have no irrelevant elaboration; they do not carry the mind away from the argument but bring a great many features of the argument to bear on the mind at once. The imagery of the opening passage represents both Reason and Religion as *light.* There is no impairment or reduction of Reason inherent in the ground of the imagery; light is traditionally a powerfully honorific image. The equation of light with

Religion and with Reason is, of course, a commonplace, but by that very fact has powerful associations. Conventional, traditional, archetypal imagery has both the accumulated force of long, civilized usage and the suggestion of ancient, original force. The power of such imagery derives in part from contexts of ritual and sacred expression where it has appeared, and in part from remoteness of origin, frequent appearance, and age-long duration. In the biblical account of creation, light is created by the first *fiat,* and elicits the first formula of divine approval: "And God saw the light, that it was good" (Genesis 1:4).

The subordination of Reason at the beginning of *Religio Laici* is subsequent to the powerfully honorific premise of the imagery, and, indeed, one of the most remarkable features of the passage is the extent of its success in subordinating Reason in spite of the honorific premise. The process begins with the association of Reason with lesser lights and Religion with the greater light and with light itself. The forms resorted to in imaging the lesser lights and in imaging the greater light must be considered, and for purposes of clarity in the outline of the full situation, there may be some advantage in beginning with the images of the greater light, Religion.

These images are: *a better Day; Day's bright Lord;* and *Supernatural Light.* The succession of *Day—Day's Lord—Light* is complicated by the fact that the second image is a metaphor which gives *Day—Sun—Light* as another form of the succession, and *Day—Monarch—Light* as still another form.[5] A particular content of the sun metaphor is designated by suggesting its rôle as a traditional symbol of monarchy. It is worth noticing, too, that the particular form of the sun-monarch image in this passage may be related to the biblical use of the sun metaphor for Christ: "I am the light of the world" (John 8:12). Whether the representation of *Day's bright Lord* ascending *our Hemisphere* is a reference to Christ's coming into the world may remain doubtful, but it is certain that the sun image of Christ and other biblical light images for God and the operation of the Holy Spirit in man are part of the relevant background of this passage; moreover, since part of the argument of the poem is that Christ's sacrifice and atonement for man's sin are a feature of the religious scheme of salvation that cannot be assimilated to a purely reasoned and natural system of religion (ll. 93-120; I, 313-14K), there is an additional reason for taking *Day's bright Lord* as a glancing reference to Christ at whose appearance Reason grows pale, disappears, *dyes, and . . . dissolves in Supernatural Light.* The sequence of images for Religion may be summarized as follows: *day-sun(monarch)-light,* with the possible addition of Christ beside sun as a tenor of the monarch metaphor and a further image of the advent of Religion in the darkling world.

The first forms resorted to in imaging the lesser power of Reason are the *borrow'd beams of Moon and Stars;* as a starting point, these are below *Supernatural Light* (which is presumably uncreated or the effluence of an uncreated essence) and below the sun (*Day's bright Lord*) which is the primary created source of light in the universe. *Borrow'd* emphasizes the fact that the light of the celestial bodies is derivative from the originally created light, and, in the case of the moon, simply reflective of the created light of the sun; the sun's light, in these ultimate terms, is also derivative, but the sun is the primary created source of light, and in the interests of the distinction which is being forged between its tenor, Religion, and the other tenor, Reason, its closeness to supernatural light is emphasized and the derivative quality of its light suppressed. *Dim* further reduces the light of moon and stars, especially by contrast to *Day's bright Lord. Rowling Fires* is a metaphor for *Moon and Stars,* not a marked step downward except that *rowling,* like *borrow'd,* emphasizes contrasting features implicit in the images of Religion, namely steadiness and control; the contrasts established call attention to multiplicity and errancy on the one hand, and to singleness and centrality on the other.[6] *Glimmering Ray* carries the subordination further by reduction to a single one of the smallest units of light, and the participle suggests unsteady, flickering, almost failing light. *Those nightly Tapers* is a metaphor for moon and stars which reduces them suddenly to candles in the night; moreover, *nightly Tapers,* a near oxymoron, calls attention to a tendency to oxymoron all through the sequence of images for Reason. For though the general ground of the imagery both for Religion and for Reason is *light,* in the former case, *light* is associated with day and in the latter case with night. The negations of the lights that are the images of Reason include *Dim, not light us here, glimmering,* and culminate on the verge of oxymoron in *nightly Tapers.* The reader will notice, too, that Reason growing pale at sight of Religion may resume the monarch metaphor by suggesting an awed subject in presence of his lawful ruler.

The relations of Reason to Religion as presented in the imagery can now be considered as they affect the soul. The passage provides a particular view of the human condition and the plight of the soul. The soul is compared to *Travellers* in darkness, *lonely, weary, wandring.* To the soul Reason is a dim light in the darkness, *lent* from above, *borrow'd* below as a guide, incapable of showing the way among the dark paths below, but capable of guiding the soul *upward to . . . Day.* With the coming of the day (Religion, divine light), Reason, the candle in the night, disappears, dissolved in the source of all light. The images of Reason, so depreciatory in direct contrast to the images of Religion, are notably appreciated and enhanced when considered in relation to the plight of the soul; Reason remains a mere instrument beside Religion which is source and end and agent, but when assigned to the soul in dark and doubtful night, the instrument takes on some luster because it is in the human context where even frail instruments are desperately necessary and valuable. Reason is essential to man until the day comes.

In summary, then, the various images and comparisons of the opening passage are a complex definition of the relations of Reason and Religion and of their value to the soul. The depreciation of Reason in contrast to Religion is very elaborate and thoroughgoing, but it is still conditioned and checked by the honorific ground of the imagery, light, which maintains, beneath all the contrasts, a fundamental continuity between the tenors, Reason and Religion, so that the former appears as the gift, effluence, and instrument of the supernatural light of which the latter is the more immediate expression. The imagery of the soul and its plight continues the emphasis on the inadequacy of Reason, but it also provides, in the context of darkness, a sharpened appreciation of the lesser instrumental light which is a guide and link to the light which is directly from God. This simultaneous valuing and disvaluing of Reason is a hallmark of the so-called Age of Reason.

In Dr. Johnson's judgment, Dryden generally excelled in the conduct of argument in verse: "When once he had engaged himself in disputation, thoughts flowed in on either side: he was now no longer at a loss; he had always objections and solutions at command: 'verbaque provisam rem'—give him matter for his verse, and he finds without difficulty verse for his matter.'[7] Dryden's generalship in verse argument arises partly from a traditional ordering array of the materials. The conception of man as occupying a middle position in a hierarchy of being led to a definition of his nature in relation to beings and qualities above and below him in the hierarchy. Such a strategy of definition invites oxymoron; both man and human reason become the focus of antithesis. Perhaps the finest formulation of such a definition of the human condition occurs in Pope's *Essay on Man*:

> Know then thyself, presume not God to scan;
> The proper study of Mankind is Man.
> Plac'd on this isthmus of a middle state,
> A being darkly wise, and rudely great:
> With too much knowledge for the Sceptic side,
> With too much weakness for the Stoic's pride,
> He hangs between; in doubt to act, or rest,
> In doubt to deem himself a God, or Beast;
> In doubt his Mind or Body to prefer,
> Born but to die, and reas'ning but to err;
> Alike in ignorance, his reason such,
> Whether he thinks too little, or too much:
> Chaos of Thought and Passion, all confus'd;
> Still by himself abus'd, or disabus'd;
> Created half to rise, and half to fall;
> Great lord of all things, yet a prey to all;
> Sole judge of Truth, in endless Error hurl'd:
> The glory, jest, and riddle of the world!

(Epistle II, ll. 1-18)[8]

Dryden too launches the argument of *Religio Laici* with an oxymoron of Reason, one which bears double fruit as the argument of the poem proceeds. The first major encounter is with the system of Deism, natural, reasoned Religion, and there the subordination of Reason comes into play, undermining the toplofty claims of finite Reason to comprehension of the Infinite and to a neat set of answers to ultimate questions. Reason, limited and criticized in the beginning, is brought to bear on the excesses of Reason. Its initial modesty confronts its extravagance:

Thus Man by his own strength to Heaven wou'd soar:
And wou'd not be Oblig'd to God for more.

(ll. 62-63; I, 313K)

Pope assailed this extravagance in similar terms:

In Pride, in reas'ning Pride, our error lies;
All quit their sphere, and rush into the skies.

(Epistle I, ll. 123-24)

Dryden, like Pope, grazes the paradox of a reasoned critique of
Reason, and directs his assault not against the use of Reason but
against the pride of Reason. In dealing with the Deist position, the
poem emphasizes the darkness in the oxymoron of Reason:

Vain, wretched Creature, how art thou misled
To think thy Wit these God-like Notions bred!
These Truths are not the product of thy Mind,
But dropt from Heaven, and of a Nobler kind.
Reveal'd Religion first inform'd thy Sight,
And *Reason* saw not, till *Faith* sprung the Light.
Hence all thy *Natural Worship* takes the *Source*:
'Tis *Revelation* what thou thinkst *Discourse*.

(ll. 64-71; I, 313K)

In dealing with a major Deist objection to the Christian position,
on the other hand, the poem emphasizes the light in the oxymoron
of Reason. The Deist objects that knowledge of a revealed religion
not revealed in all times and all places to all men cannot reasonably
and justly be made an essential and universally applied condition
of salvation. The answer to the objection represents in itself a reasoned deviation from strict interpretation of a Christian doctrine,
and the mode of salvation proposed for those who had not the
benefit of Revelation is by way of the right use of the natural light of
Reason:

They, who the written Rule had never known,
Were to themselves both Rule and Law alone:
To Natures plain indictment they shall plead;
And, by their Conscience, be condemn'd or freed.
Most righteous Doom! because a *Rule reveal'd*
Is *none* to *Those*, from whom it was *conceal'd*.
Then those who follow'd *Reasons* Dictates right;
Liv'd up, and lifted high their *Natural Light;*

63

With *Socrates* may see their Maker's Face,
While Thousand *Rubrick-Martyrs* want a place.

(ll. 202-11; I, 316K)

The poem, in reasoning its objection to the reasoned system of Deism, confronts pride with modesty. The mask of modesty is also employed in formulating the answer to the major Deist objection to the Christian position, and in this case modesty reveals a tincture of pride in a churchman and a church doctrine. The treatment of Athanasius is a skillful blending of modesty with maintained force of criticism:

> Nor does it baulk my *Charity*, to find
> Th' *Egyptian* Bishop of another mind:
> For, though his *Creed Eternal Truth* contains,
> 'Tis hard for *Man* to doom to *endless pains*
> All who believ'd not all, his Zeal requir'd;
> Unless he first cou'd prove he was inspir'd.
> Then let us either think he meant to say
> *This Faith,* where *publish'd,* was the onely way;
> Or else conclude that, *Arius* to confute,
> The good old Man, too eager in dispute,
> Flew high; and as his *Christian* Fury rose
> Damn'd all for *Hereticks* who durst *oppose.*

(ll. 212-23; I, 316-17K)

Modesty advances under the emblem of charity, but the emblem becomes an effective weapon against the strictness of Athanasius. There is something less than charity in the smooth accuracy of the reference to *th' Egyptian Bishop;* it is the failure to say *Christian* that is damaging, along with the just perceptible Old Testament aura that attends upon Egyptian. *Zeal* is another subtly corrosive word because of its close association with pretentious or irresponsible religious enthusiasm.[9] The face of charity, under cover of ostensible indulgence, is always half turned away from Athanasius; he is termed *good,* but the goodness is adulterated with treacherous indulgence in the phrase *the good old Man.* When the term *Christian* is finally applied to Athanasius, it appears in the ironic oxymoron of *his Christian Fury.* Modesty is the lens which reduces Athanasius by magnifying his pride. Like proud man who, by his own strength, would soar to heaven, Athanasius is represented as one who *flew high.*

64

The moderate voice of the poem consistently seeks to hold the oxymoron of Reason in a balanced position and thereby to criticize those who have proudly ignored the darkness of Reason or willfully abjured or cut off its light. In its discussion of the authority of the scriptural text and of written and oral tradition, the poem carefully treads a *via media,* acknowledging the defects revealed by the light of Reason in the argument of a literal and perfect scriptural authority, and seeing, by the light of Reason, the fallibility of tradition and of professedly infallible interpretation of scripture and tradition. But the poem also insists on the adequacy of scripture and the usefulness of tradition. From the beginning of the poem, Reason and Revelation have been related as forms of light, and in this section of the poem, although the adequacy of Revelation is asserted, the usefulness of Reason is also asserted in the presence of the historical impairment of Revelation:

> Thus, *first Traditions* were a proof alone;
> Cou'd we be *certain* such they *were,* so *known*:
> But since some Flaws in long descent may be,
> They make not *Truth* but *Probability.*
> Even *Arius* and *Pelagius* durst provoke
> To what the *Centuries preceding* spoke.
> Such difference is there in an oft-told Tale:
> But Truth by its own Sinews will prevail.
> *Tradition written* therefore more commends
> *Authority,* than what from *Voice* descends:
> And this, as perfect as its kind can be,
> Rouls down to us the Sacred History:
> Which, from the *Universal Church receiv'd,*
> Is *try'd,* and *after,* for its *self* believ'd.
>
> (ll. 342-55; I, 320K)

From this middle position the poem, continuing under the mask of modesty, assails the errors of the extremes, the monolithic authoritarianism which the Church had interposed between the Scriptures and the private man's Reason, and the pluralistic confusion which resulted from the sectarian exaltation of the private spirit and denigration of learning. The poem distinguishes these two errors as pride and ignorance, but pride and presumption are objects of attack in both cases. The Church had been presumptuous in claiming an exclusive authority to interpret and in keeping the layman from direct contact with Revelation. The sects, throwing off a proud and learned authority, have transferred presumption from clergy to laity and put a foolish face of pride upon private inspiration and ignorance. It is the bright side of the oxymoron of Reason that undergirds the middle position between authority and inspiration and reveals the errors of both extremes.

This is the poem's account of the darkness imposed by authority, and of the interruption of that darkness by the light of rational inquiry:

> In times o'ergrown with Rust and Ignorance,
> A gainfull Trade their Clergy did advance:
> When want of Learning kept the *Laymen* low,
> And none but *Priests* were *Authoriz'd* to *know*:
> When what small Knowledge was, in them did dwell;
> And he a *God* who cou'd but *Reade* or *Spell;*
> Then *Mother Church* did mightily prevail:
> She parcel'd out the Bible by *retail*:
> But still *expounded* what She *sold* or *gave;*
> To keep it in *her Power* to *Damn* and *Save*:
> *Scripture* was *scarce,* and as the Market went,
> Poor *Laymen* took *Salvation* on *Content;*
> As needy men take Money, good or bad:
> *God's* Word they had not, but the *Priests* they had.
> Yet, whate'er *false Conveyances* they made,
> The *Lawyer* still was *certain* to be paid.
> In those dark times they learn'd their knack so well,
> That by long use they grew *Infallible*:
> At last, a knowing Age began t' enquire
> If *they* the *Book,* or *That* did *them* inspire:
> And, making narrower search they found, thô late,
> That what they thought the *Priest's,* was *Their* Estate:
> Taught by the *Will produc'd,* (the written Word)
> How long they had been *cheated* on *Record.*
> Then, every man who saw the Title fair,
> Claim'd a Child's part, and put in for a Share:
> Consulted Soberly his private good;
> And sav'd himself as cheap as e'er he cou'd.

(ll. 370-97; I, 320-21K)

One kind of darkness is dissipated when the light of Reason leads man once more up to the light of Revelation. Man is *taught by the Will produc'd, (the written Word)*.

The poem proceeds to represent the unfortunately continuous movement from darkness in the absence of light to a dark bedazzlement in the presence of light, and describes a new kind of presumption:

> 'Tis true, my Friend, (and far be Flattery hence)
> This good had full as bad a Consequence:
> The Book thus put in every vulgar hand,
> Which each presum'd he best cou'd understand,
> The *Common Rule* was made the *common Prey;*
> And at the mercy of the *Rabble* lay.
> The tender Page with horney Fists was gaul'd;
> And he was gifted most that loudest baul'd:
> The *Spirit* gave the *Doctoral Degree:* ⎫
> And every member of a *Company* ⎬
> Was of *his Trade,* and of the *Bible free.* ⎭
> Plain *Truths* enough for needfull *use* they found;
> But men wou'd still be itching to *expound:*
> Each was ambitious of th' obscurest place,
> No measure ta'n from *Knowledge,* all from GRACE.
> *Study* and *Pains* were now no more their Care;
> *Texts* were explain'd by *Fasting,* and by *Prayer:*
> This was the Fruit the *private Spirit* brought;
> Occasion'd by *great Zeal,* and *little Thought.*
> While Crouds unlearn'd, with rude Devotion warm,
> About the Sacred Viands buz and swarm,
> The *Fly-blown Text* creates a *crawling Brood;*
> And turns to *Maggots* what was meant for *Food.*
> *A Thousand daily Sects rise up, and dye;*
> *A Thousand more the perish'd Race supply.*
> So all we make of Heavens discover'd Will
> Is, not to have it, or to use it ill.
> The Danger's much the same; on several Shelves
> If *others* wreck *us,* or *we* wreck our *selves.*
>
> (ll. 398-426; I, 321-22K)

The danger into which the license of the private spirit leads is represented as a peril equal to that arising from authority. The sameness of the two dangers is emphasized by the use of commercial images for both; the commercial images used to describe the pre-

Reformation condition are carried on without a break into the post-Reformation condition. The conduct of the authoritarian church is rendered in scathing images of trade:

> Then *Mother Church* did mightily prevail:
> She parcel'd out the Bible by *retail*:
> But still *expounded* what She *sold* or *gave;*
> To keep it in *her Power* to *Damn* and *Save*:
> *Scripture* was *scarce,* and as the Market went,
> Poor *Laymen* took *Salvation* on *Content.*

The commercial stain spreads over the Reformation and the private spirit:

> Then, every man who saw the Title fair,
> Claim'd a Child's part, and put in for a Share:
> Consulted Soberly his private good;
> And sav'd himself as cheap as e'er he cou'd.

Both critical attacks are made swiftly and stoutly effective by the jangling conjunctions, *Bible* and *retail, Scripture* and *Market, cheap* and *sav'd.* The ironic appearance of *Mother Church* as tradesman and venal lawyer reducing the Bible to an article of sale and legal manipulation, and exacting all the traffic would bear, is matched by the Puritan collocation of trade and Bible; the sacred text, no longer parceled out by the few, becomes the trade of the many, and is represented as food corrupted by swarms of flies. The emphasis of the imagery surrounding the Puritan commercialization is not on the exaction of money but on vulgarization. The sacred text is depraved and treated as common, and commonness is presented on a scale of imagery which ranges swiftly downward from the *horney Fists* of an insensitive, *unlearn'd,* bawling *Rabble, rude* and *itching,* to loathsome and prolific insects that *buz and swarm, a crawling Brood* that fly-blow the sacred *Food* and turn it to *Maggots.*

The use of commercial images to represent errors of authority and the private spirit in the religious sphere is continuous with part of the earlier attack on Deism. The Deist's error is different, of course, in that he has not abused but denied Revelation; he has not reduced the Bible to an article of trade, but he is represented as having reduced the whole intercourse between man and God to the level of a commercial transaction:

This *general Worship* is to PRAISE, and PRAY:
One part to *borrow* Blessings, one to *pay*.

(ll. 50-51; I, 312K)

In this couplet the faulty light of Reason is represented as conceiving the relationship of man to God in commercial terms, the borrowing occurring at the instigation of presumptuous man and not as the generous and original lending by God, and man further presuming to pay for what he gets. The ignominious *quid pro quo* is given the damagingly ironic presentation which the couplet form can manage so adroitly; the rhyme equation of *PRAY-pay* (highlighted further by the typographical distinction) mirrors the Deist's (and Reason's) misconception. The ironic *mésalliance* is presented also by the alliterative equation in *borrow Blessings*.[10]

All of these commercial images are related to and removed from the center of God's generous lending established in the opening lines of the poem. The idea of paying for blessings, the practice of selling salvation, the effort to purchase salvation as cheaply as possible are all affronts to God, the Giver, from whom all blessings freely flow and who has given His Son, celestial wealth, to pay the otherwise unpayable price. The commercial imagery of the poem presents the mean departures from and venal corruptions of the relationship rendered initially in the borrowing of light lent from above until the advent of *Day's bright Lord*.[11]

Religio Laici exhibits Dryden's capacity in a middle kind of writing that faces in neither the satiric nor the encomiastic direction but devotes itself to creating a moderate and appealing voice of instruction. D. Nichol Smith's tentative observation that the poem may contain less imagery than is usual in Dryden's poems is certainly borne out by a study of the poem's imagery;[12] not only is there less imagery, but there is also something special about the way in which imagery is employed to attend upon the argument, walking the middle path of discrimination, dispensing both praise and blame. The fact that this poem, with less than the usual amount of imagery, begins with an outpouring of images has already been noticed.[13] A rationale of this anomaly in terms of the generalship of the argument has been suggested, but there remains the question that has been held in abeyance of seeing the anomaly as it relates to the full fabric of

69

the poem's imagery, and to the management of the middle style. Does the poem absorb the anomaly, or is its obtrusiveness made to subserve a complete design? Certainly the obtrusiveness of the opening passage is emphasized rather than muted by the concluding lines of the poem which present themselves bluntly bare of images:

> Thus have I made my own Opinions clear:
> Yet neither Praise expect, nor Censure fear:
> And this unpolish'd, rugged Verse, I chose;
> As fittest for Discourse, and nearest Prose:
> For, while from *Sacred Truth* I do not swerve,
> *Tom Sternhold's* or *Tom Shadwell's Rhimes* will serve.
>
> (ll. 451-56; I, 322K)

The middle style of the poem, as it pertains to imagery, is not a matter of an all-pervasive modesty in the use of images, but of a fine modulation between the richness of the opening and the bareness of the conclusion. From the floodtide of the beginning the movement of the imagery is steadily recessive until at the end of the poem the beach is bare. The floodtide of the beginning occurs together with and as an expression of the celestial lights which dominate the poem, the supernatural and original light of Religion and the derived light of Reason. It is under the influence of Revelation that the imagery of the poem touches its high-water mark, and the attenuations of light which are introduced immediately in the account of the rôle of Reason are the beginning of the recessive movement in the imagery. The argument moves from its *donnée* of supernatural light to the confrontation of systems of thought and of institutions in the context of human history which have pretended either to provide an equivalent for or to transmit this light, and the strongest assemblage of images late in the poem characterizes various kinds of darkness which have been blots on religious history; it is proper that Reason, the attenuated light, should be made to conduct itself modestly, and that its various discursive explorations produce no blaze of glory—"the Figurative way is for the Passions"—in the imagery. The imagery is made to render back the initially established derivativeness of Reason by the repetition of images which derive from the opening passage; for the imagery as well as for the argument, the opening passage is a dominating revelation. The argument of the poem is thus stretched upon its own oxymoron of the darkness and light of Reason. Between Reason's most

70

legitimate pride, its relationship to supernatural light, and the modesty incumbent upon Reason immersed in the human condition, lies the movement of the imagery of the poem. In the concluding passage the modesty of Reason and of poetry are signalized by the disappearance of imagery. There is only the simplicity of the reference to *Sacred Truth* (which no translation into other terms can finally dim —not even Tom Sternhold's psalms) to recall the light that was in the beginning.

NOTES

1. *Lectures on Dryden* (Cambridge, 1914), p. 155.

2. *Diary, Reminiscences, and Correspondence of Henry Crabb Robinson,* ed. Thomas Sadler (2 vols., Boston, 1870), II, 292.

3. *Lives of the Poets,* ed. G. B. Hill (3 vols., Oxford, 1905), I, 442.

4. Professor Douglas Bush has noticed that Dryden's comparison of Reason to the dim light of moon and stars is the same as Donne's in *Biathanatos— Science and English Poetry: A Historical Sketch, 1590-1950* (Oxford, 1950), p. 49.

5. The sequence of creation as it appears in Genesis moves downward from light. Dryden's lines move in the reverse direction, gaining thereby an effect of climax, carrying the tenor, Religion, to the source of light. The monarch metaphor for the sun as ruler of the day appears in Genesis 1:16 and 18; the monarch metaphor is there also applied to the lesser light, but this image the poem sets aside.

6. *Rowling Fires,* of course, reflects the Greek source of the term "planet," which means "wandering."

7. *Lives of the Poets,* I, 459.

8. Quotations from Pope's poetry are from *The Poems of Alexander Pope,* ed. John Butt (Twickenham Ed., 6 vols., London and Oxford).

9. Pope's *Essay on Man* (Epistle III, ll. 261-62) offers the same conjunction of terms:

Zeal then, not charity, became the guide,
And hell was built on spite, and heav'n on pride.

10. See W. K. Wimsatt's article, "One Relation of Rhyme to Reason: Alexander Pope," *Modern Language Quarterly,* V (1944), 323-39, for a discussion of some of these resources of couplet form.

11. The poem's linkage of religious and commercial language has been commented on by McD. Emslie in the course of a more general discussion of Dryden's imagery, "Dryden's Couplets: Imagery Vowed to Poverty," *The Critical Quarterly,* II (1960), 51-57. The general argument of this article perhaps tends to collapse distinctions among modes of imaging in the diverse kinds of poems that Dryden wrote.

12. *John Dryden* (Cambridge, 1950), p. 61.

13. Professor Smith notices this exception to his general observation about the imagery of the poem (p. 61).

IV

Absalom and Achitophel

 *ELIGIO LAICI* served to present a kind of poetry and a method of imagery different in many respects from the prologues and epilogues; *Religio Laici* is a middle kind of verse discourse lying between satire and praise. *Absalom and Achitophel* (1681) is also a poem distinct in kind from those heretofore discussed, and although it is usually designated a satiric poem, it has affinities with both the satiric and the laudatory prologues and epilogues. Written to be read, not delivered from the stage, this poem is distinguished from the short pieces for the theater by its length and narrative method, but from the point of view of imagery there are close connections. The translation of particular personages and particular sequences of events into the value order is one of the offices performed by imagery in this poem as it was in those pieces for the theater. *Absalom and Achitophel* is a notable and a complex instance of such a translation, containing both the satiric drive toward disvalue, and the complimentary drive toward value.

Si Propiùs stes/ Te Capiet Magis (If you stand closer, you will be more taken by it)—this motto, from Horace's *Ars Poetica,* Dryden affixed to *Absalom and Achitophel.* The motto can be interpreted in several ways, but it seems certainly to point to the contemporary persons and events which are represented in the poem. From this point of view, the poem's Jewish history is a veil to be pierced so that the features of English history beneath the veil may be traced in detail. This is a necessary undertaking. The poem is involved with two histories, Jewish and English, and the persons and incidents of both must be known. The analogies that are implicit in the identities of the poem must be made explicit. Once the details have been recognized, however, the fact of the comparison should not be forgotten. The poem's implicit assertion is that one history is like another. This assertion is basically a valuative assertion of the sort that is present in the parallels of Plutarch's *Lives,* but the implicit nature of this assertion in Dryden's poem gives the matter another turn.

By being about two histories at once, *Absalom and Achitophel* is about neither. Jewish history is modified to fit English history, and English history modified to fit Jewish history; as a result, the action of the poem is a *tertium quid,* removed from the specifications of both histories and, in an important sense, not history at all. For example:

He to his Brother gives Supreme Command;
To you a Legacy of Barren Land:
Perhaps th' old Harp, on which he thrums his Layes:
Or some dull *Hebrew* Ballad in your Praise.

(ll. 437-40; I, 228K)

The reference to a brother is appropriate to Charles, rather than to David; the harp and the ballad are more clearly appropriate to David than to Charles. Or, to take another case, the Sanhedrin is employed in the poem as a metaphor of Parliament, but the Sanhedrin does not belong to the history of David's reign.

In his preface Dryden disclaimed the rôle of inventor and claimed that of historian: *"Were I the Inventour, who am only the Historian . . ."* (I, 216K). This disclaimer, however, is merely part of the thin pretense that the poem is sheer Jewish history based on Second Samuel. It is a gesture of modesty over the designedly evident fact of the invention exhibited in the combination of the two histories.[1*] Moreover, the use of Jewish history emphasizes the valuative aspect of the history that is drawn from a sacred book. The whole Judaeo-Christian tradition has operated to transmute the history of the Jews into a moral order. By fastening a set of English persons and a sequence of English events to a set of Jewish persons and a sequence of Jewish events, Dryden has set English history in a moral order. The imagery of the poem extends this moral order beyond what is supplied by Second Samuel; the imagery is extended to embody the full moral order of Christian theology, and it is in terms of that moral order that a part of English history is judged. The imagery creates the intersection of "never and always" with "then and in England."

Notes for this chapter begin on page 90.

The direction which the imagery of the poem takes in bringing to bear the full Christian order is suggested in some of the statements in Dryden's preface: *"But, since the most excellent Natures are always the most easy; and, as being such, are the soonest perverted by ill Counsels, especially when baited with Fame and Glory; 'tis no more a wonder that he withstood not the temptations of* Achitophel, *than it was for* Adam, *not to have resisted the two Devils; the Serpent, and the Woman. . . . Were I the Inventour . . . I shoud certainly conclude the Piece, with the Reconcilement of* Absalom *to* David. . . . *I have not, so much as an uncharitable Wish against* Achitophel; *but, am content to be Accus'd of a good natur'd Errour; and, to hope with* Origen, *that the Devil himself may, at last, be sav'd. . . . God is infinitely merciful; and his Vicegerent is only not so, because he is not Infinite"* (I, 216K). An examination of passages from the poem will show that the imagery takes up the themes of God and man, the devil and the fall, the temptation of Adam and the temptation of Christ; perhaps the most important feature of the imagery is the superimposing of two themes in the David-Absalom relationship; the theme of God and Adam, and the theme of God, the Father, and His beloved Son, Christ.

The imagery of the poem at an early stage introduces faint suggestions of David as God and of Absalom as Adam and of the events in paradise:

> What e'r he did was done with so much ease,
> In him alone, 'twas Natural to please.
> His motions all accompanied with grace;
> And *Paradise* was open'd in his face.
> With secret Joy, indulgent *David* view'd
> His Youthfull Image in his Son renew'd:
> To all his wishes Nothing he deny'd,
> And made the Charming *Annabel* his Bride.
>
> (ll. 27-34; I, 217K)[2]

It is worth noticing that the account of David given in the lines following the passage quoted above continues to hover near the aspect of David as God:

> Thus Prais'd, and Lov'd, the Noble Youth remain'd,
> While *David,* undisturb'd, in *Sion* raign'd.
>
> (ll. 41-42; I, 218K)

Sion, of course, refers quite specifically to the hill upon which David's royal palace was built, and the metonymy which takes Sion for the whole of Israel is frequent in the Bible; Sion, however, is also frequently applied to the heavenly city of God, a metaphoric application which it shares with the name Jerusalem.

The imagery, in dealing with the stirrings of rebellion against Israel's monarch, presses more insistently the duality of David as king and as God, and it also subsumes the populace in Adam's rebellion:

> The *Jews*, a Headstrong, Moody, Murmuring race,
> As ever try'd th' extent and stretch of grace;
> God's pamper'd people whom, debauch'd with ease,
> No King could govern, nor no God could please;
> (Gods they had tri'd of every shape and size
> That God-smiths could produce, or Priests devise:)
> These *Adam*-wits, too fortunately free,
> Began to dream they wanted libertie.
>
> .   .   .   .
>
> Those very *Jewes*, who, at their very best,
> Their Humour more than Loyalty exprest,
> Now, wondred why, so long, they had obey'd
> An Idoll Monarch which their hands had made:
> Thought they might ruine him they could create;
> Or melt him to that Golden Calf, a State.
>
> (ll. 45-52, 61-66; I, 218K)

In both of the above passages the imagery involves the political ruler with the divine ruler, and involves rebellion against the earthly king with idolatry; the first passage connects rebellion against the earthly king with Adam's rebellion against a divine restraint. *State,* which is the contemporary term for a polity distinct from a true monarchy, is given the metaphor of religious idolatry and error, the golden calf. The nature of the imagery here makes it seem possible that the reference in a later passage is different from or additional to what a series of editors, Sir Walter Scott, George R. Noyes, and James Kinsley, have suggested; the lines in question are:

> The *Jews* well know their power: e'r *Saul* they Chose,
> God was their King, and God they durst Depose.
>
> (ll. 417-18; I, 227K)

75

Professor Noyes has the following note on the second line of the couplet: "Alluding to the Commonwealth 'without a king,' established in 1649, which is compared to the condition of Israel under the Judges. It was brought to an end by the creation of the Protectorate under Cromwell (*Saul*) in 1653."[3] Professor Kinsley, in his edition, simply cites a note by Scott which Noyes may well have been following. An expression so forceful and unqualified as *God was their King* may, of course, be aimed at the political cant of the Commonwealth period, but the direct mention of deposition in the latter half of the line suggests an allusion to Charles I, the last ruler in the sacramental succession before the interruption of that succession by the Commonwealth and by the rule of Cromwell, the popularly chosen as opposed to the divinely made ruler. In any case, the deposition of God refers to the interruption of rule by divine right, an interruption which occurred at the execution of Charles I and was merely affirmed in the choice of Cromwell as Protector. It was this interruption of the succession that made it possible for *the Jews* to regard Charles II as *An Idoll Monarch which their hands had made*.

The stirrings of unrest against David (Charles II) are directly linked, by way of the imagery, with unrest in Eden fanned and directed by the Devil:

> But, when to Sin our byast Nature leans,
> The carefull Devil is still at hand with means;
> And providently Pimps for ill desires:
> The Good old Cause reviv'd, a Plot requires.
> Plots, true or false, are necessary things,
> To raise up Common-wealths, and ruin Kings.

(ll. 79-84; I, 219K)

At the level of particulars, the *Good old Cause* that is being revived is the cause of the Commonwealth against Charles I,[4] and the Devil who is at hand with means is the Earl of Shaftesbury; in terms of imagery, the *Good old Cause* is perhaps hinted to be Satan's rebellion against God, and the plot, the Hell-engendered design against man in Eden. At any rate, political unrest is here given the image of original sin encouraged and enabled by the Devil, and the ruin of Charles II corresponds to Satan's purposed discomfiture of his eternal enemy, God.

"Dryden," Professor Verrall remarks, "was . . . profoundly original. The Biblical parallel is used *to admit the 'heroic style.' "*[5] Imagery suggestive of *Paradise Lost* is consistently applied to those who have risen against the king or who are plotting a new uprising:

> Some had in Courts been Great, and thrown from thence,
> Like Feinds, were harden'd in Impenitence.
>
> (ll. 144-45; I, 220K)

The crucial rôle of the imagery in passages such as this needs to be stressed. Take away the simile, and *Courts, thrown,* and *Impenitence* bury themselves in historical events; the court of the English king dismisses certain disaffected persons, and away from the court their disaffection hardens. The identification of English with Jewish history, of course, prevents this sheer particularism; what might otherwise be merely local is raised a notch to a generalization within history: "Disaffected persons become fixed in their disloyalty away from court." Only with the simile, *like Feinds,* does the full force of *Impenitence* come into operation; with this image, *Courts* takes on a bright luster which carries over to *thence,* so that *thrown from thence* has a pinnacle of reference from which the fall is epic, Satan's and Vulcan's, the full enlargement of the Miltonic context with the impenitence hardened in Hell. It is the image, *like Feinds,* that refers history to judgment, "never and always."

The portrait of Achitophel which follows in lines 150-203 has been much admired, especially because it holds a residue of qualification and fairness that largely overcomes the stigma of mere faction. Achitophel is represented as sagacious, bold, a fiery soul, a great wit, blest with wealth and honor; he is praised especially as a judge with discerning eyes and clean hands, ready without the stimulus of bribery or special pleading to redress the grievances of the wretched, "Swift of Dispatch, and easie of Access." The fairness of the portrait lies in the presentation of all sides of a many-sided man and in a willingness to recognize the rôle of contingency in shaping Achitophel's actions. The mitigations of the portrait are the mitigations possible with respect to a person of high qualifications in any particular historical situation. The portrait, however, also wears another and sterner aspect; among all the qualifications and mitigations there is steadily present the aspect of judgment, and the full verdict of that judgment appears in the imagery applied to Achitophel in this passage and in later sections of the poem.

The imagery of the portrait sets the mitigations in a different light by pressing down upon Achitophel the image of Satan, another figure of high qualifications and mitigated in his evil nature by some remnant glories:

> he above the rest
> In shape and gesture proudly eminent
> Stood like a Towr; his form had yet not lost
> All her Original brightness, nor appear'd
> Less then Arch Angel ruind . . .
>
> . . . .
>
> Dark'n'd so, yet shon
> Above them all th' Arch Angel.[6]

The opening lines of the portrait are blunt enough, so blunt that the unstressed metaphor of the second line is easily missed:

> Of these the false *Achitophel* was first:
> A Name to all succeeding Ages Curst.
>
> (ll. 150-51; I, 220-21K)

The name that is cursed for all succeeding ages is Achitophel, but it is not only Achitophel. More light is shed on the full identity of Achitophel later in the portrait in lines such as these:

> In Friendship False, Implacable in Hate:
> Resolv'd to Ruine or to Rule the State.
> To Compass this the Triple Bond he broke;
> The Pillars of the publick Safety shook:
> And fitted *Israel* for a Foreign Yoke.
>
> (ll. 173-77; I, 221K)

Implacable in Hate echoes the defiance of Milton's Satan pledging "study of revenge, immortal hate" (*P. L.*, I, l. 107). The resolution to rule or ruin is a close reflection of the Satanic determination expressed in Beelzebub's address setting forth the project against God's creation:

> either with Hell fire
> To waste his whole Creation, or possess
> All as our own. . . .
>
> (*P. L.*, II, ll. 364-66)

And though the next three lines return us unmistakably to history (both Second Samuel and Restoration England), it is still a history with reverberations. The breaking of *the Triple Bond*, referring at the level of then and in England to the triple alliance formed in 1668 among England, Sweden, and the Dutch Republic against France, an alliance which Shaftesbury played a prominent part in breaking up, parallels on another level the action that Satan had to undertake to carry out his design against mankind:

> at last appeer
> Hell bounds high reaching to the horrid Roof,
> And thrice threefold the Gates; three folds were Brass,
> Three Iron, three of Adamantine Rock,
> Impenitrable. . . .
>
> (*P. L.*, II, ll. 643-47)

Likewise, across the description of Achitophel's son, reflecting historically the contempt in which he was held and Plato's definition of man (*implumis bipes*), flits perhaps the shadow of Milton's Chaos, and of another son:

> And all to leave, what with his Toyl he won,
> To that unfeather'd, two Leg'd thing, a Son:
> Got, while his Soul did hudled Notions try;
> And born a shapeless Lump, like Anarchy.
>
> (ll. 169-72; I, 221K)
>
> The other shape,
> If shape it might be call'd that shape had none
> Distinguishable in member, joynt, or limb.
>
> (*P. L.*, II, ll. 666-68) [7]

And there is a further suggestion of Satan and a strong suggestion of Eden in the final lines:

> Oh, had he been content to serve the Crown,
> With vertues only proper to the Gown;
> Or, had the rankness of the Soyl been freed
> From Cockle, that opprest the Noble seed:
> *David*, for him his tunefull Harp had strung,
> And Heaven had wanted one Immortal song.
> But wilde Ambition loves to slide, not stand;
> And Fortunes Ice prefers to Vertues Land:

Achitophel, grown weary to possess
A lawfull Fame, and lazy Happiness;
Disdain'd the Golden fruit to gather free,
And lent the Croud his Arm to shake the Tree.

(ll. 192-203; I, 222K)

Whatever weight we may be willing to give to any of these allusions individually, it is difficult not to feel that collectively they fill the portrait in: the *Name to all succeeding Ages Curst* is *Satan,* and the action which the imagery has gradually supplied to the portrait is the action of Satan's emergence from Hell for his attempt upon Eden. With all its mitigations, all its fairness at the level of representation of a gifted man, the judgment that the portrait holds over its subject is that he is the intrepid Devil himself emerging from Hell to destroy Eden and to devote man to death.

Dr. Johnson found fault with the lapses in what he seems to have regarded as a simple parallelism of two histories: "The original structure of the poem was defective: allegories drawn to great length will always break; Charles could not run continually parallel with David."[8] The poem, however, as has been suggested earlier, is neither Jewish history nor English history but a *tertium quid,* an action somewhere between or above both histories and commenting on both. The imagery is *relevant* to both histories, but the images are designed and made *appropriate* in terms of the *tertium quid,* the fundamental action of the poem. There are instances where particulars of English history are related to particulars of Jewish history without resort to imagery; in these cases the action of the poem is simply not given a symbolic embodiment. The symbolic embodiment, the action in the imagery, rises above and dominates the whole mass of the particulars of both histories, but without appearing concretely in significant relation to each particular as it occurs. An occasional connection between Jewish history and English history with no image of God or Satan or Eden or Hell or Heaven can be accepted because the multiplicity of such connections *accompanied by* such images adequately establishes the general symbolic action; in the same way, a connection that specifically involves one but not both histories with the symbolic pattern can be accepted because the multiplicity of triple connections has adequately related both histories to the general symbolic action. In cases of the former type, historical parallels are prominent and the symbolic action distant; in cases of the latter type, the symbolic action is dominant. The former is more occupied with history and the latter more with value. The office performed by the imagery, as has been said earlier, is to provide an emblem of and residence for value.

The section of the poem which follows the portrait of Achitophel has been generally referred to by critics as "The Temptation of Absalom." In this section the imagery presents two major themes in combination, or superimposed upon one another: the theme of the temptation in the Garden and the theme of the temptation of Christ. The connection which the imagery makes between Absalom's and Adam's rebellion has already been pointed out as a suggestion in a passage of Dryden's preface and in several passages of the poem. In the section of the poem now to be considered, the Absalom-Adam relation is made unmistakable with the setting of the temptation partly in the context of the Garden; the imagery applied to Achitophel is the imagery of Satan as he appeared in the Garden, the arguments employed by Achitophel are a blend of Satan's arguments in the Garden and his arguments to Christ in the desert, and—the most important consideration—the event of the temptation is a fall. The Absalom-Christ relation is pressed by the images of Savior and Messiah applied to Absalom, and by the main theme of the temptation, power over one of the kingdoms of this world.

In Achitophel's first address to Absalom, the tempter is associated with an aspect of the Garden and Absalom is given the images of the Messiah:

> Him [Absalom] he attempts, with studied Arts to please,
> And sheds his Venome, in such words as these.
>   Auspicious Prince! at whose Nativity
> Some Royal Planet rul'd the Southern sky;
> Thy longing Countries Darling and Desire;
> Their cloudy Pillar, and their guardian Fire:
> Their second *Moses,* whose extended Wand
> Divides the Seas, and shews the promis'd Land:
> Whose dawning Day, in every distant age,
> Has exercis'd the Sacred Prophets rage:
> The Peoples Prayer, the glad Deviners Theam,

81

The Young-mens Vision, and the Old mens Dream!
Thee, *Saviour,* Thee, the Nations Vows confess;
And, never satisfi'd with seeing, bless.

(ll. 228-41; I, 223K)[9]

It should be noticed, moreover, that Achitophel's argument occasionally adopts the form of Satan's argument in *Paradise Regained*. The following passage is part of Achitophel's argument:

Our Fortune rolls, as from a smooth Descent,
And, from the first Impression, takes the Bent:
But, if unseiz'd, she glides away like wind;
And leaves repenting Folly far behind.
Now, now she meets you, with a glorious prize,
And spreads her Locks before her as she flies.
Had thus Old *David,* from whose Loyns you spring,
Not dar'd, when Fortune call'd him, to be King,
At *Gath* an Exile he might still remain,
And heavens Anointing Oyle had been in vain.

(ll. 256-65; I, 223K)

The following lines are a part of Satan's argument in Book III of *Paradise Regained*:

thy Kingdom though foretold
By Prophet or by Angel, unless thou
Endeavour, as thy Father *David* did,
Thou never shalt obtain; prediction still
In all things, and all men, supposes means,
Without means us'd, what it predicts revokes.[10]

(III, ll. 351-56)

The Messianic token, Davidic lineage, appears as an authorizing phrase and as the Devil's flattery in both passages. Absalom's reply to Achitophel's first approach may be compared with part of Christ's reply to Satan in *Paradise Regained*. Absalom says:

My Father Governs with unquestion'd Right;
The Faiths Defender, and Mankinds Delight:
Good, Gracious, Just, observant of the Laws;
And Heav'n by Wonders has Espous'd his Cause.
Whom has he Wrong'd in all his Peaceful Reign?
Who sues for Justice to his Throne in Vain?
What Millions has he Pardon'd of his Foes,

82

Whom Just Revenge did to his Wrath expose?
Mild, Easy, Humble, Studious of our Good;
Enclin'd to Mercy, and averse from Blood.[11]

(ll. 317-26; I, 225K)

Christ retorts to Satan's objection of the glory required by God of men:

And reason; since his word all things produc'd,
Though chiefly not for glory as prime end,
But to shew forth his goodness, and impart
His good communicable to every soul
Freely; of whom what could he less expect
Then glory and benediction, that is thanks,
The slightest, easiest, readiest recompence
From them who could return him nothing else,
And not returning that would likeliest render
Contempt instead, dishonour, obloquy?

(*P. R.*, III, ll. 122-31)

These passages from *Paradise Regained* are not cited in an attempt to establish verbal parallels. They are cited simply to show that the identities suggested in the imagery of the poem, Satan for Achitophel and Christ for Absalom, are supported by the similarity in the arguments and sentiments expressed by Satan and Achitophel, Absalom and Christ. The significant difference between Absalom and Christ is that Absalom is the Messiah primarily in the mouth of Achitophel and of the people, a false Christ set up by Satan and accepted by the deceived populace, whereas Christ, rejected of men, is indeed the Son of God. At a later point in the poem, popular acceptance of Absalom as the Messiah is emphasized:

The Croud, (that still believe their Kings oppress)
With lifted hands their young *Messiah* bless.

(ll. 727-28; I, 235K)

The Messianic and Satanic imagery is, indeed, quite unmistakable in the poem. It is worth remarking that even Achitophel uses Satanic imagery; making brazenness do the work of guile, he applies Satanic imagery to David:

He is not now, as when on *Jordan's* Sand
The Joyfull People throng'd to see him Land,
Cov'ring the *Beach*, and blackning all the *Strand*:

83

> But, like the Prince of Angels from his height,
> Comes tumbling downward with diminish'd light.
>
> (ll. 270-74; I, 224K)

In this fashion Achitophel compounds falsehood and deception, creating false images both of the Messiah and of Satan, false pictures of both good and evil. In yielding to the temptation of Achitophel, in being deceived, Absalom shows that he is not the true son; he reverts to the status of Adam whose fall put an end to man's residence in Eden.

Absalom weakens and Achitophel triumphs; the imagery is primarily of the Garden:

> Why am I Scanted by a Niggard Birth?
> My Soul Disclaims the Kindred of her Earth:
> And made for Empire, Whispers me within;
> Desire of Greatness is a Godlike Sin.
> Him Staggering so when Hells dire Agent found,
> While fainting Vertue scarce maintain'd her Ground,
> He pours fresh Forces in, and thus Replies:
> Th' Eternal God Supreamly Good and Wise,
> Imparts not these Prodigious Gifts in vain;
> What Wonders are Reserv'd to bless your Reign?[12]
>
> (ll. 369-78; I, 226K)

The special merit of the imagery is its functional character. The imagery points, on the one hand, to an Absalom (Adam) too much taken with his half-claim to royalty (a god-like nature) and desiring to be king (as a god), and, on the other hand, to an Achitophel playing upon Absalom's half-claim and desire by addressing him as the true son (Christ) and promising him dominion over one of the kingdoms of this world. The duality in the imagery applied to Absalom is impressive because it embodies the fact of his nature (man) and the nature of his temptation (to be more). His salvation lies in obedience and is the dear hope of David (as Monmouth's restoration to dutifulness was of Charles)—an earned sonship, a true sonship, is available to him. The epic accent introduced by the imagery lends to Absalom's choice the significance of Adam's.

Apart from the imagery employed in the portrait of Achitophel and the temptation of Absalom, there is a liberal sprinkling of anti-

God imagery throughout the poem. The metaphor of David, God's anointed king, conditions the use of anti-God imagery for David's enemies; David himself characterizes his enemies in anti-God terms in his speech from the throne:

> Their *Belial* with their *Belzebub* will fight.
>
> (l. 1016; I, 243K)

Shimei, one of the enemies of David, is represented as fostering anti-God forces:

> During his [Shimei's] Office, Treason was no Crime.
> The Sons of *Belial* had a glorious Time.
>
> (ll. 597-98; I, 232K)

The extension of the anti-God imagery to include anti-Christ imagery is conditioned by the fundamental departure from the Second Samuel context which is involved in the Messianic imagery. The Messianic imagery is within the Old Testament frame, but verges upon the actual New Testament Messiah (and the Christ of *Paradise Regained*). The anti-Christ imagery introduces New Testament contexts. There are, for example, suggestions of the Pharisees as the New Testament represents them in the portrait of Shimei:

> *Shimei*, whose Youth did early Promise bring
> Of Zeal to God, and Hatred to his King;
> Did wisely from Expensive Sins refrain,
> And never broke the Sabbath, but for Gain.
>
> (ll. 585-88; I, 232K)

The New Testament context is unmistakably employed to create an anti-Christ portrait by skillful parody:

> For *Shimei*, though not prodigal of pelf,
> Yet lov'd his wicked Neighbour as himself:
> When two or three were gather'd to declaim ⎤
> Against the Monarch of *Jerusalem*,   ⎬
> *Shimei* was always in the midst of them. ⎦
> And, if they Curst the King when he was by,
> Woud rather Curse, than break good Company.
>
> (ll. 599-605; I, 232K)

The blasphemy of Shimei's coupled piety and acquisitiveness is effectively conveyed by a series of turns upon the language of various

New Testament passages (notably Matthew 22:39 and 18:20) which artfully image the perversion.

The anti-God and anti-Christ forces have their stronghold in Jerusalem (London):

> But he [Jonas], tho bad, is follow'd by a worse,
> The wretch, who Heavens Annointed dar'd to Curse.
>
> .   .   .   .
>
> The City, to reward his [Shimei's] pious Hate
> Against his Master, chose him Magistrate.
>
> (ll. 583-84, 593-94; I, 232K)

The populace, having tried *Gods . . . of every shape and size,* unsteady, fickle, "humourous" rather than loyal, are represented as governed by the moon, and the imagery develops this emblem as a *leitmotiv* of the crowd, varying it in the related images of ebbing and flowing tides and pressing the lunar implications of inconstancy and madness:

> For, govern'd by the *Moon,* the giddy *Jews*
> Tread the same track when she the Prime renews:
> And once in twenty Years, their Scribes Record,
> By natural Instinct they change their Lord.
>
> (ll. 216-19; I, 222K)
>
> What Standard is there in a fickle rout,
> Which, flowing to the mark, runs faster out?
> Nor only Crowds, but Sanhedrins may be
> Infected with this publick Lunacy.
>
> (ll. 785-88; I, 237K)

The final section of the poem swings from Jerusalem and David's opposition to the stalwart few who have bulwarked the throne, and to David himself speaking from the throne. The movement is from satire to praise, and, in the landscape of England, from London to Oxford.

Dr. Johnson criticized adversely the concluding section of *Absalom and Achitophel;* his objection runs as follows: "As an approach to historical truth was necessary the action and catastrophe were not in the poet's power; there is therefore an unpleasing disproportion between the beginning and the end. We are alarmed by a faction formed out of many sects various in their principles, but agreeing in their purpose of mischief, formidable for their numbers, and strong by their supports, while the king's friends are few and weak. The chiefs on either part are set forth to view; but when expectation is at the height the king makes a speech, and 'Henceforth a series of new times began.' Who can forbear to think of an enchanted castle, with a wide moat and lofty battlements, walls of marble and gates of brass, which vanishes at once into air when the destined knight blows his horn before it?"[13] Dr. Johnson admits that what affects him as a "disproportion between the beginning and the end" was in some sort thrust upon Dryden by the historical facts. Charles II's carefully managed surprise dissolution of the Oxford Parliament had set the opposition members clamoring for horses and scurrying out of Tory Oxford. The King's opposition was discomfited and scattered quite as if the destined knight had blown his horn. There is, moreover, beyond the historical facts, a consideration of some weight that rests upon the action in the imagery of the poem. The symbolic identity of the destined knight needs to be appreciated:

> With all these loads of Injuries opprest,
> And long revolving, in his carefull Breast,
> Th' event of things; at last his patience tir'd,
> Thus from his Royal Throne by Heav'n inspir'd,
> The God-like *David* spoke: with awfull fear
> His Train their Maker in their Master hear.
>
> Thus long have I, by native mercy sway'd,
> My wrongs dissembl'd, my revenge delay'd:
>
> .   .   .   .
>
> Must I at length the Sword of Justice draw?
> Oh curst Effects of necessary Law!
> How ill my Fear they by my Mercy scan,
> Beware the Fury of a Patient Man.
> Law they require, let Law then shew her Face;
> They coud not be content to look on Grace,
> Her hinder parts, but with a daring Eye
> To tempt the terror of her Front, and Dye.
>
> .   .   .   .
>
> Their *Belial* with their *Belzebub* will fight;
> Thus on my Foes, my Foes shall do me Right:
>
> .   .   .   .
>
> Henceforth a Series of new time began,
> The mighty Years in long Procession ran:

Once more the Godlike *David* was Restor'd,
And willing Nations knew their Lawfull Lord.[14]

(ll. 933-40, 1002-09, 1016-17, 1028-31; I, 241-43K)

The symbolic matrix in which David is stoutly set for this final speech is clearly that of the acts and utterances of God. The context that may be invoked is the sixth book of *Paradise Lost* where God, after the indeterminacy of the struggle between his angels and Satan's host, on the third day takes effective action through his Son. The ease with which the rout of Satan's army is then accomplished is well known. Dr. Johnson's comment needs to be considered in relation to this symbolic action. His estimate of the opposition is just: "a faction formed out of many sects . . . agreeing in their purpose of mischief, formidable for their numbers, and strong by their supports." Dr. Johnson, however, underestimates the king; he speaks only of his supports: "the king's friends are few and weak."[15] The imagery enforces the consideration that symbolically this is the very King for whom gates of brass lift up their heads and bars of iron yield. In terms of the action in the imagery, "the destined knight" who appears as a *deus ex machina* is the very God. The imagery, therefore, makes the balance between the King and his enemies more equal and calls in question what Dr. Johnson termed the "unpleasing disproportion between the beginning and the end." The critical problem that arises has an affinity with that posed by the Savior's single-handed defeat of Satan and his host in *Paradise Lost*. The remarkable and perhaps aesthetically improbable fact of Charles II's victory is made akin to God's victory over Satan; the imagery works to translate an unlikely historical event into value terms and thereby to lay hold on a greater aesthetic probability.

The action embodied in the imagery of *Absalom and Achitophel* turns upon the basic metaphor of the Garden, Eden, for the kingdom. Shakespeare, for one, had employed this metaphor for the kingdom and, in *Richard II,* devoted a full scene (Act III, scene 4) to the symbolic consideration of the king as gardener. Gaunt, in his famous speech (Act II, scene 1) speaks of England as "This other Eden, demi-Paradise." In the local condition of Denmark, Hamlet sees the state of the world and exclaims, " 'Tis an unweeded garden" (Act I, scene 2). In Dryden's poem the kingdom is a paradise that may be lost and that may be regained. As it is man's—that is to say, as it is

Charles II's and David's, Monmouth's and Absalom's, as it is Adam's
—it is subject to loss; as the Garden is God's and man's and Satan
is in it, the Garden hovers between being lost by man's action or
saved by God's action. The evil attempt upon the Garden is at the
center of the poem. The historical personages, the human beings at
the base of the action, give the metaphor of Adam a pervasive
validity; there is an Adam assimilated to Satan in Achitophel, an
Adam who falls in Absalom, and an unfallen Adam presiding over
the Garden in David. On the other hand, the imagery of the Messiah
that Achitophel applies to Absalom, false and guileful as the application is, points to an identity that, in the realm of value, is potential
in the true son of David, and points beyond that to the identity potential in his father, David, the Maker in the master.

Absalom and Achitophel is a complex poem. The variety of its
elements is not satisfactorily contained under the tent of satire, and
there is a good deal to be said for Professor Verrall's suggestion that
the poem be classified as an *"epyllion, or epic in miniature, compris-
ing satiric elements."*[16] Such a classification can more easily assimilate
the main facts about the poem which the present study of its imagery
suggests: the presence of an epic action adumbrated in considerable
detail by imagery in the heroic style, and the presence together in one
poem of a focus of satire in London (the populace stirred up by
Achitophel and Absalom) and a focus of praise in the king (David's
speech from the throne fortified by the historical event of Charles II's
speech at Oxford); both images of the king are here, the image of the
king threatened and long-suffering and the image of the king asserting his power and triumphant. The difficulty which Dr. Johnson
found in reconciling the strength of the king's enemies with the king's
sudden overpowering success is not quite resolved by considering it at
the level of imagery, but translated to this level of the poem, Johnson's objection sheds new light. The phase of the epic action adumbrated in the London section of the poem is truncated; there is a
Fall, but the consequences to Adam and to Eden are suspended. At
the point of truncation a second phase of the epic action is adumbrated, the rout of Satan and his hosts by God. It may be that Dryden
should be censured for cramming the frame of an "epic in miniature"
with two phases of an epic action which, in their new context and

arrangement, will not submit to a neat joint. It may also be that such a critical demand misconceives the nature of a miniature epic; such a form must shrink or truncate the epic action, and it seems to have been Dryden's strategy, as the imagery suggests, to present certain epic panels, the parts of one large painting conveying the significant moments of an action, not the full continuity of the action.[17] In the first line of the poem there is a suggestion of romance epic, a suggestion of the fabulous: "In pious times, e'r Priest-craft did begin." Dr. Johnson caught this same suggestion when he described the king as appearing at the end like the destined knight at the blast of whose horn the enchanted castle vanishes into air. It is really a very old aesthetic problem; the king threatened or deposed is credible, the king enthroned and ideal appears fabulous. "Fled is that music:— Do I wake or sleep?"—London and our world always seem real; Oxford and Eden (and the nightingale) seem myths.

NOTES

1. Dryden, of course, was not the first to make the connection between Jewish and English history. An anonymous Catholic poem, *Naboth's Vineyard,* had appeared in 1679, and in 1680 an anonymous tract, *Absalom's Conspiracy, or The Tragedy of Treason,* was published. In "The Originality of *Absalom and Achitophel," Modern Language Notes,* XLVI (1931), 211-18, R. F. Jones has shown that the application of the life of King David to English political situations began early in the seventeenth century. Jones points out that Nathanael Carpenter's *Achitophel, or the Picture of a Wicked Politician,* published in 1627, attained a sixth edition by 1641. This work drew the character of Achitophel and applied the portrait especially to Catholic figures involved in political intrigue, but Achitophel soon became a byword for a wicked politician and was freely employed, especially in sermons, by both Puritans and Royalists.

2. Line 30, with its mention of paradise, Dryden seems to have recalled in a more detailed evocation of Eden in *To Her Grace The Dutchess of Ormond*:

Whose Face is Paradise, but fenc'd from Sin:
For God in either Eye has plac'd a Cherubin.

(ll. 155-56; IV, 1467K)

3. *The Poetical Works of John Dryden,* ed. George R. Noyes (Cambridge Ed., Boston [1909, 1937] 1950), p. 960, n. to l. 418.

4. Professor Noyes' note on the passage gives the following explanation: "*Good Old Cause.* That is, of the Commonwealth; Dryden's aim is to identify the Whigs with the men who rebelled against Charles I. There is, possibly, a more specific reference to the intrigues between Charles I and the Presby-

terians and the parliament in 1647-48, which led ultimately to the execution of the king and the establishment of the Commonwealth" (p. 958, n. to l. 82).

5. *Lectures on Dryden* (Cambridge, 1914), p. 57.

6. *Paradise Lost,* I, ll. 589-93, 599-600; quotations from Milton are from *The Poetical Works of John Milton,* ed. H. C. Beeching (Oxford, 1935).

7. Professor Morris Freedman's article, "Dryden's Miniature Epic," *Journal of English and Germanic Philology,* LVII (1958), 211-19, argues for the probable functional allusion to *Paradise Lost* here and in other instances I have cited. Only in a minority of cases does my interpretation of the function of these allusions diverge from his.

8. *Lives of the Poets,* ed. G. B. Hill (3 vols., Oxford, 1905), I, 436-37.

9. Line 239 is an echo of the beginning of the apocalyptic section of Joel (2:28) which has sometimes been regarded as foreshadowing a Messianic kingdom.

10. Professor A. B. Chambers' note, "Absalom and Achitophel: Christ and Satan," *Modern Language Notes,* LXXIV (1959), 592-96, calls attention to the relevance of *Paradise Regained* to Dryden's handling of the temptation scene and suggests something of the dual Adam-Christ rôle of Absalom.

11. *Mankinds Delight,* in the second line of this passage, is referred by Professor Noyes (p. 960) to Suetonius' *amor ac deliciae generis humani* applied to the Emperor Titus. Perhaps the phrase may also be referred to the psalmist's injunctions to delight in the Lord, Psalms 1:2 and 37:4; see also Job 34:9 and Isaiah 58:14.

12. Professor Verrall noticed the Miltonic context invoked in these lines and pointed to the Miltonic inversion in l. 373 (*Him Staggering so when Hells dire Agent found*) as a clear suggestion of Milton's Satan—*Lectures on Dryden,* p. 55.

13. *Lives of the Poets,* I, 437. Dryden has *time,* not *times* as quoted by Dr. Johnson.

14. Professor Noyes' note on ll. 1006 ff. (p. 963) is pertinent: "Moses on Mount Sinai was not allowed to behold the face of the Lord, 'For there shall no man see me, and live'; he was permitted, however, to see the 'back parts' of the Lord (Exodus XXXIII. 20-23). Dryden here terms Grace the *hinder parts* of Law: the Whigs have clamored for Law against the Catholics and denied the king's power to grant pardon; hence they shall behold the face of Law and die themselves."

15. *Lives of the Poets,* I, 437.

16. *Lectures on Dryden,* p. 59.

17. Ruth Wallerstein has suggested that both *Mac Flecknoe* and *Absalom and Achitophel* have a kind of parallel in Renaissance painting, particularly in the Triumph paintings and in such group portraits as Lucas Cranach's "Woman Taken in Adultery" where the construction is simple and where the portraits present typical attitudes—"To Madness Near Allied: Shaftesbury and His Place in the Design and Thought of *Absalom and Achitophel,*" *Huntington Library Quarterly,* VI (1943), 448.

V

To Mr. Oldham and To Anne Killigrew

HE CONCENTRATION upon praise which characterizes the conclusion of *Absalom and Achitophel* suggests a broader consideration of Dryden's ways of using imagery in poems particularly devoted to praise. Since the objects of praise are various, and since the compositions addressed to different objects are written in different keys, one may expect differences to appear in the treatment of images. It is provisionally useful to describe a range in the conventional objects of praise comprising the praise of men, especially famous men and their achievements; the praise of something like an incarnation, that is, of god-like achievements or an idea, principle, or ideal under the form of man; and the praise of God, the hymn to the all-achieving and perfect. Dryden's elegy *To Mr. Oldham* is praise of a man; Dryden's ode *To Anne Killigrew,* more than praise of a woman, is praise of a type of incarnation.[1]* In both poems a mournful elegiac movement qualifies the movement of praise, but this qualification, serious and part of the limiting frame in the praise of Oldham, is both more serious and more lightened, drastic but relieved, in the praise of a type of incarnation. Because of the dual nature of the object of praise in the ode *To Anne Killigrew,* the elegiac movement is simply a phase of the total movement and is a limiting frame only for the object as person; in its other aspect, as transfigured being and incarnate principle, the object of praise from the beginning surmounts death and mourning.

To Mr. Oldham is a poem made to honor an achievement and to lament an early death. It is not a long poem and remains much

*Notes for this chapter begin on page 128.

closer to its occasioning person than does the ode *To Anne Killigrew;* the difference between the Killigrew ode and the Oldham elegy, so far as imagery is concerned, is all the difference between imagery creating an apotheosized figure and imagery elevating but not translating a human figure. The two poems are remote from each other in the treatment of images, though both are examples of the rhetoric of praise. *To Mr. Oldham* is so undemonstrative in the use of imagery that it appears at first to have a style close to the deliberative style of *Religio Laici.*

Dryden's elegy adopts the conventional metaphor of departure for death, and the lines are spoken as one poet's farewell to another. For several lines the poem emphasizes the closeness of these two poets, and then, by way of an image, arrives at their sameness:

> For sure our Souls were near ally'd; and thine
> Cast in the same Poetick mould with mine.
>
> (ll. 3-4; I, 389K)[2]

The next image emerges out of sameness to the presentation of the two once more as distinct:

> To the same Goal did both our Studies drive,
> The last set out the soonest did arrive.
>
> (ll. 7-8)

This couplet is still dominated by *Studies,* the tenor of the discussion. *Goal* is certainly inconspicuous as metaphor, and the second line of the couplet, though it makes the image more definite, scarcely makes it emphatic. The second line, however, does make the two persons distinct and is an easy approach to the image which becomes emphatic in the classical allusion in the next couplet, where the two poets are compared to Nisus and Euryalus, runners in an epic race. The speaker in the poem, complimenting Oldham with having won the poetic race, represents himself as Nisus, who fell, and Oldham as young Euryalus, who won the race. The comparison also involves the fact that the competitors in the race are, in both cases, friends, and since the epic account of Nisus and Euryalus achieves the status of an *exemplum* of friendship, the competitive element in the image of the race is modified by the allusion. The race image appearing in the allusion to the *Aeneid* is the first major image that Dryden has put in the poem.

The second major image follows close upon that of the race, and is mainly remarkable as a contrasting image. Oldham's career has been seen through an image of speed and striving, though in an atmosphere of friendship. The second image, which is carried out at some length, regards Oldham's poetry as fruit *early ripe* and his poetic production as an *abundant store*. This image is resumed and concluded in a triplet:

> Thy generous fruits, though gather'd ere their prime
> Still shew'd a quickness; and maturing time
> But mellows what we write to the dull sweets of Rime.

(ll. 19-21)

The metaphor of Oldham as a tree, though not expressed, is fully implied, so that the two major images of the poem present the sharp contrast of the racing figure, running for the prize, and the planted tree, bearing abundant fruit. One is bound to remark the juxtaposition of an image of running and striving with an image of a slow and gradual natural process of maturation, the former emphasizing effort, discipline, and competition in the poetic career, the latter an easy, natural, unwilled growth and maturing of powers. Taken together, these two images contrive to emphasize both aspects of poetic ability, what is learned and achieved—Art—and what is native and given—Nature.

The one striking note of accord between the two images is struck by the term *quickness* applied to Oldham's poetic fruits. This term, together with the initial *early ripe,* imports qualities appropriate to the race into the imagery of natural growth; the natural process is represented as unusually rapid (*early ripe*), and *quickness* is the kind of term that helps to strengthen the suggestion since it is a word so readily applicable to the race image. As applied here to fruits, of course, *quickness* has the basic meaning of "quick maturing," but the meaning of "sharpness, caustic quality," which the word had as applied to fruits and also to speech and writing, may impinge here upon the metaphor of Oldham's poetic production, along with the suggestion of growth advanced far enough, though not fully matured, to have attained characteristics of independent life. The suggestion of a degree of accord between the dominantly opposed images, the deliberate involvement together of contrasting images, serves to maintain awareness of the fundamental situation in which natural gifts and achieved powers are allied.

To Mr. Oldham contains two allusions, the one already mentioned to the Nisus and Euryalus episode in Book V of the *Aeneid,* and an allusion near the end of the poem to Marcellus (who appears in Book VI of the *Aeneid*) :

> Once more, hail and farewel; farewel thou young,
> But ah too short, *Marcellus* of our Tongue;
> Thy Brows with Ivy, and with Laurels bound;
> But Fate and gloomy Night encompass thee around.
>
> (ll. 22-25)

The allusion to Nisus and Euryalus has the form of a simile; the allusion to Marcellus is a metaphor. There is an effect of progression in moving from simile to metaphor, first comparing Oldham to, then identifying him with, a classical figure. The concluding couplet above emphasizes the fact that the allusion to Marcellus is designed to have its circuit through the *Aeneid* by closely echoing part of Virgil's description of the young Marcellus:

> Sed nox atra caput tristi circumvolat umbra.[3]

In Dryden's translation of the *Aeneid,* published thirteen years after the poem to Oldham, the line is rendered thus:

> But hov'ring Mists around his Brows are spread,
> And Night, with sable Shades, involves his Head.
>
> (*Aeneis,* VI, ll. 1198-99; III, 1232K)

One notices, however, that in Dryden's lines, Oldham is presented as a victor as well as a figure encompassed by fate and gloomy night; so far as Dryden's poem is concerned, this representation of the laureled victor resumes and concludes the imagery of the race. He has been represented as a victor in the race for poetic achievement, and *Marcellus of our Tongue* is a metaphor clearly designed to suggest this conquest of language. The line from the *Aeneid* which Dryden directly echoes contains no suggestion of Marcellus as victor, and Dryden has altered it to introduce the note of victory; in Virgil's description black night is around the brows of young Marcellus, but in Dryden's description the brows are bound with ivy and with laurels so that an antithesis is set up within the couplet between the laureled victor and the encompassing night. The note of victory, not struck by Virgil in the line which Dryden has directly imitated, is struck, however, in Virgil's account of the young Marcellus as he allies him with the "great" Marcellus. The line which Dryden echoes is from Virgil's account of the young Marcellus, the nephew of Augustus, whom Virgil presents together with Marcus Claudius Marcellus (ca. 268-208 B. C.), one of the Roman generals during the Second Punic War, the conqueror of Syracuse and the military leader who for the third and last time in Roman history won the *spolia opima,* a man who was called "the sword of Rome." Between "great Marcellus" and the young Marcellus Virgil establishes a close relationship:

> *Aeneas,* here, beheld of Form Divine
> A Godlike Youth, in glitt'ring Armour shine:
> With great *Marcellus* keeping equal pace;
> But gloomy were his Eyes, dejected was his Face:
> He saw, and, wond'ring, ask'd his airy Guide,
> What, and of whence was he, who press'd the Hero's side?
> His Son, or one of his Illustrious Name,
> How like the former, and almost the same:
> Observe the Crowds that compass him around;
> All gaze, and all admire, and raise a shouting sound.
>
> .   .   .   .
>
> No Youth shall equal hopes of Glory give:
> No Youth afford so great a Cause to grieve.
> The *Trojan* Honour, and the *Roman* Boast;
> Admir'd when living, and Ador'd when lost!
> Mirror of ancient Faith in early Youth!
> Undaunted Worth, Inviolable Truth!
> No Foe unpunish'd in the fighting Field,
> Shall dare thee Foot to Foot, with Sword and Shield.
> Much less, in Arms oppose thy matchless Force,
> When thy sharp Spurs shall urge thy foaming Horse.
> Ah, cou'dst thou break through Fates severe Decree,
> A new *Marcellus* shall arise in thee!
>
> (*Aeneis,* VI, ll. 1188-97, 1210-21; III, 1232K)

Virgil does a good deal to identify the young Marcellus with the great Marcellus, but though he insists upon their likeness and surrounds the young man with acclaim and the tokens of greatness, the distance between promise and fulfillment is also a feature of the relationship. For the young Marcellus there are *hopes of Glory* rather than an achieved glory, and *Fates severe Decree* interposes to prevent the younger man from achieving full status as *a new Marcellus.* Dryden's allusion, in *To Mr. Oldham,* is primarily to the young Marcellus untimely cut off, and to this Marcellus as giving promise of the triumphs of the great Marcellus but prevented by fate. However, since in the lines where the Marcellus allusion appears Dryden's image of the race is concluded with the presentation of the young poet as an *actual* victor, and since *Marcellus of our Tongue* is a metaphor suggesting command and conquest, it is apparent that the allusion plays upon Virgil's young Marcellus at the limits of his approach to the great Marcellus, and accordingly involves both the young Marcellus and the great and victorious Marcellus in the final representation of Oldham. In Virgil's picture of the young Marcellus, the antithesis is drawn between his promise and his fate, whereas in Dryden's allusion to Marcellus, the antithesis is drawn between achievement and fate.

The end of Dryden's poem is like a classical medallion struck for "the English Juvenal." There is a superb finish to the final couplet which both distinguishes and coalesces achievement and death, victory and defeat, the great Marcellus and the young Marcellus. The lines are held apart by *but,* which insures the distinction of their purport, but they are drawn together by the parallelism between the circlet of ivy and laurel and the larger encompassing circle of fate and gloomy night; the imagery makes the glory of it and the pity of it concentric and coincident. The imagery of the race and the imagery of the natural cycle have here their end, illuminating the use of the conventional, classical *hail and farewel.* Honor to the victor and the victor's debt to nature are paid at once.

To Mr. Oldham is a special case of the spare and intensive use of imagery in the rhetoric of praise. The severity of the limitation on imagery in this poem means that each of the two major images must be a bearing timber of the structure. Accordingly, one image is made to carry the theme of man's will and achievement, the theme of purpose and Art, and the other image is made to carry the theme of man's fate, the theme of destiny and Nature. These themes, exfoliating from the two main images, are directly related to the basic movement and countermovement of elegy in which praise of the dead is modulated into praise of the victor, the natural defeat modulated into the achieved victory. It is, in fact, a special quality of this poem that the conclusion manages to make the movement of death circle around the attitude of victory, creating a final counterpoise of man's will and man's fate, of Art and Nature.

T. S. Eliot has observed of this elegy that "the lack of suggestiveness is compensated by the satisfying completeness of the statement"; and of Dryden's style in general that "his words . . . are precise, they state immensely."[4] It is the concentration of a great deal of meaning in a pair of images and in the relationship between them, and the close articulation of these images with epic allusions that make possible, in this elegy, an extraordinarily economical accomplishment. Imagery establishes the general qualities and conditions of the man and the career that are being praised, and allusions extend the reference of these qualities and conditions by affiliating them with an epic activity and with an epic posture. The allusions are compact importations of episodes, and since they enlarge the man and his career by bringing them into contact with epic figures and situations, they are, in effect, generalizing, pulling the poem away from the particularities of Oldham's career, but at the same time epitomizing, by referring Oldham's career to permanent symbols of epic. There is a stoic limitation to the reach of this generalizing of the object of praise; the reach is only for such permanence as time has. Man's achievement and fate are rendered in terms of the Grecian urn world of epic figures and epic attitudes. The dominion of Nature is modified by the qualified permanence of the symbols of Art, but the reiterated *farewel* strikes with an accent like Keats' "forlorn." It is in poems of praise where the object of praise is enlarged beyond the frame of Nature and epic that conclusion strikes with quite a different note, not the tolling of a bell but the pealing of many bells.

Dryden's remarks in his preface to *Eleonora* give some idea of the principles of his practice in poems like the ode *To Anne Killigrew*: *"And on all Occasions of Praise, if we take the Ancients for our Patterns, we are bound by Prescription to employ the magnificence of Words, and the force of Figures, to adorn the sublimity of Thoughts.* Isocrates *amongst the* Grecian *Orators; and* Cicero, *and the younger* Pliny, *amongst the* Romans, *have left us their Precedents for our security: For I think I need not mention the inimitable* Pindar, *who stretches on these Pinnions out of sight, and is carried upward, as it were, into another World"* (II, 583K). In the ode *To Anne Killigrew,* Dryden, having an occasion for praise, employs imagery that carries the poem *upward, as it were, into another World.* The imagery helps to create and define the fundamental thematic movement of the ode. The imagery which characterizes Anne Killigrew as an object of praise carries the main themes of the poem, and the dramatic action in which the imagery engages Anne develops these themes in a particular way. Anne Killigrew is not treated as a static object of praise, but is established and made active in relation to the poet who addresses her. In Stanza IV the poet turns from direct address to Anne Killigrew to direct and prayerful address to God in the course of which the imagery explicitly assigns to Anne the rôle for which all that is attributed to her in the poem qualifies her. The mode of direct address to Anne does not return until the very end of the poem. Accordingly, the thought of the poem is conducted by talking initially to Anne Killigrew, then by talking to God about Anne Killigrew, thereafter, without overt indication of the shift, by talking to others, an assumed audience, about Anne, and finally by direct address to Anne, as in the beginning, so that a rhetorical cycle is completed. The imagery of Stanza IV, where the prayerful address to God occurs, indicates what the conversation of the poem is about:

> O Gracious God! How far have we
> Prophan'd thy Heav'nly Gift of Poesy?
> Made prostitute and profligate the Muse,
> Debas'd to each obscene and impious use,
> Whose Harmony was first ordain'd Above
> For Tongues of Angels, and for Hymns of Love?
> O wretched We! why were we hurry'd down
> This lubrique and adult'rate age,
> (Nay added fat Pollutions of our own)
> T' increase the steaming Ordures of the Stage?
> What can we say t' excuse our *Second Fall?*
> Let this thy *Vestal,* Heav'n, attone for all!

Her *Arethusian* Stream remains unsoil'd,
Unmixt with Forreign Filth, and undefil'd,
Her Wit was more than Man, her Innocence a Child!

(ll. 56-70; I, 461K)

The three preceding stanzas of direct address to Anne have established by their imagery a character qualified to appear in the prayer of the supplicant, sinful poet as one having merit to atone for the particular sins which he acknowledges for himself and other poets, and for which he here entreats divine forgiveness. The rest of the poem sets forth the earthly career and merits of the atoning personage and the poet concludes by addressing her directly and explicitly as a saint.

The particular sins acknowledged in Stanza IV and the terms in which they are acknowledged should be observed closely. The poet acknowledges abuse and misuse of poetry, which is referred to in images of God's *Heav'nly Gift* and of *the Muse*. The imagery offers two statements, or two ways of saying the same thing: that God's *Heav'nly Gift of Poesy* has been *prophan'd*, and that *the Muse* has been debauched, *made prostitute and profligate*. The two statements, or two elements of one statement, are both important because the poem employs their terms as alike or equivalent here and elsewhere. The imagery of the former is Christian, the imagery of the latter classical. *The Muse* is alien in the context of a Christian prayer. It is clear enough in this case that *the Muse* is to a very considerable extent assimilated in the Christian context, first, by being used in direct connection with God's *Heav'nly Gift of Poesy,* and, second, by being accorded a *Harmony . . . first ordain'd Above/ For Tongues of Angels, and for Hymns of Love.* The presence of the image of *the Muse,* however, complicates the poetic situation. So far as sheer statement is concerned, *Poesy* and *the Stage* and *the Muse* stand together as the art which is imaged as morally fallen. *The Muse,* however, goes beyond *Poesy* and *the Stage* in suggesting that the fall involves the debasement of the classical ideal.

The fact that the fall has been aesthetic as well as moral and the suggestion that it has involved debauching the classical ideal help to account for the imagery used to characterize the atoning figure. *Thy Vestal, Heav'n* is an interesting case of the possibility of identity between Christian and classical terms; *Vestal* is a term used of nuns,

100

and this application of the term is here enforced by the connection with *Heav'n* as well as by the fact that the first stanza of the poem uses imagery that refers to Anne Killigrew unequivocally as a nun. The classical significance of *Vestal,* however, cannot be ignored, especially with *Arethusian* following in the next line. *Vestal,* in the classical sense, refers to a virgin consecrated to tending the sacred fire in the temple of Vesta, and the image is employed here in the general sense of one consecrated to the sacred fire, a moral guardian and symbol, extended to include the preservation of poetry by *Arethusian* in the following line.[5] The atoning figure, like the fall for which she is invoked, is presented in the double aspect of Christian and classical; she is imaged as a nun whose virgin life fits the pattern of a religious atonement for fallen man, and she is a vestal virgin whose *Arethusian Stream* may atone for fallen poets and a fallen poetry. It is the primary conceit of the poem to regard the religious and the aesthetic atonement as one action performed by one atoning figure; attention to the imagery reveals the two strands of the action, but reveals them woven together all through the poem, and often as tightly involved as they are in the image *Vestal.*

In the fourth stanza, as in the rest of the poem, imagery works to elevate statement and action from a local and particular meaning toward a universal and general meaning. On this occasion of praise, the innocence of Anne Killigrew's life and the purity of her poetry are the points from which the poem starts. What begins as the salutary effect of Anne Killigrew's life and poetry upon the corruption of the Restoration stage is carried upward, in the fourth stanza, toward the greater action of atonement for the fall. To manage this translation the poem is bound to establish as many congruities as possible between the corruption of the stage and the fall, and between the figure of Anne Killigrew and a traditional atoning figure. The corruption of the stage is imaged as profanation of a *Heav'nly Gift* and debasement of a *Harmony . . . first ordain'd Above;* these images are appropriate to the original as well as to this *Second Fall.* Anne Killigrew is imaged as Heaven's *Vestal,* an image which is appropriate to her as virgin and as poet, and parallel with the imagery of the initial stanza which has characterized her as a nun. The imagery of Anne as *Vestal* is elaborated by metaphorizing her poetic purity as an *Arethusian Stream . . . unsoil'd,/ Unmixt with Forreign Filth, and undefil'd,* and by metaphorizing her wit as *more than Man* and her innocence as *a Child;* these images are appropriate to Anne as a pastoral poet, feminine and gifted with a superior wit and with a childlike innocence. Appropriate to Anne, these images are also congruent with the traditional atoning figure. In her wit that is *more than Man* she is like Christ the Redeemer, and in her innocence like the Christ-child. The imagery by no means insists upon these relationships, but suggests just enough to make the atoning figure quietly present. The imagery points and moves the figure of Anne Killigrew toward another world.

An examination of the imagery of Stanzas I-III of the ode will show how Anne Killigrew is prepared for her appearance in the poet's prayer as an atoning virgin with suggestions of the Virgin and of the traditional Atonement; in the imagery of Stanzas V-X the process of justifying, supporting, enriching, and explicating the metaphorical treatment of Anne Killigrew is carried on to its climax and conclusion. Professor E. M. W. Tillyard has observed: "Dryden knew that, when in the first stanza of his *Ode* he speculated on the heavenly region where Anne Killigrew's soul might inhabit, every educated reader would know that he was recalling, though in Christian terms, Virgil's speculations at the beginning of the *Georgics* on where the apotheosised Augustus would have his heavenly seat."[6] Professor Tillyard has commented further on the extent to which the medieval world picture, fundamental and structural in the imagery and thematic design of much Elizabethan poetry, dramatic and non-dramatic, remains intact in Dryden's poem as a ground of the imagery: "His account of the various regions of the eternal heavens where the soul of Anne Killigrew might inhabit is as precise as anything in *Orchestra*. She has left the regions of mutability below the moon; she may be in a planet (comparatively close to the earth); she may be in the region of the fixed stars and circle with the great host of heaven; or she may be called to 'more superior bliss,' farther from earth and nearer to God, in the empyrean."[7] Professor Tillyard's remarks call attention to the combination, in this stanza, of Christian and classical elements, and this combination is the same as that discussed in the case of Stanza IV. It is a combination that deserves, here and elsewhere in the poem, detailed consideration. The specula-

tive pondering of where Anne Killigrew has her heavenly seat proceeds from regions just beyond the sway of mutability to the region
of *the vast Abyss* trod by the seraphim and close to God in the
empyrean. The imagery ascends, in terms of the traditional medieval
and Christian world picture, moving Anne Killigrew toward the
upper heavens, speculatively and diffidently but nonetheless effectively enlarging with each step the metaphorical possibilities of Anne
Killigrew. An air of diffidence actually facilitates the poetic business
of this stanza which is the translation of Anne Killigrew to a celestial
position. This initial translation is one of the anchors of the poem; it
is to Anne Killigrew established in this position that the prayer in
Stanza IV refers. The basis for assigning her a place with the blest
has, however, a special aspect; there is more here than the simple
translation to bliss of a pure soul. This soul has been taken up into
Heaven because blessed *and because accomplished;* she is welcome
in Heaven for her poetry. There is a lot of imagery in the stanza defining Anne Killigrew as a pure and chaste soul—*Youngest Virgin-
Daughter of the Skies,* for example, and *made in the last Promotion
of the Blest* with *Palmes, new pluckt from Paradise* as well as the
images at the end of the stanza, *Inmate, young Probationer, Candi-
date of Heav'n* which wrap Anne Killigrew in the white garb of a
nun and invest her with the merits of a conventual life. The imagery
establishes a course of merit of a kind traditionally associated with
the salvation of a saint or a nun, and proceeds to make the merits
special and attractive by the addition of poetry. Anne's poetry is
imaged as the *first Fruits* given by her, the sacrifice which opens the
way to Heaven. *Virgin-Daughter of the Skies,* however, and *Palmes*
and *Celestial Song* and the contrast to *a Mortal Muse* taken together
with the general emphasis on poetry also move Anne closer to the
classical idea of a muse, one of the virgin-daughters of Jupiter to
whom the palm tree was sacred. The imagery assumes the double
part of asserting the sanctification of the poetess as a virgin, a nun,
one of the blest, and of suggesting the apotheosis of a poetess as a
heavenly muse. The state of blessedness is a state of harmony in
which the good and the beautiful are closely allied. In this Heaven the
medieval system and the classical ideal are enshrined together.

The imagery of the first stanza is definitely focused upon Heaven,
and upon Anne Killigrew's place there, but since the concluding

lines of the stanza appeal to Anne to attend to *a Mortal Muse,* the poet of the ode, whose verse is akin to the verse practiced by Anne on earth, the mortal career of Anne has been introduced into the poem and linked by way of its poetic occupation to another mortal. The second stanza begins on this note of mortality, but in the process of considering the beginning of Anne's career, the whole matter of her origin and the origin of her poetry, the stanza moves back into Heaven. The primary locus of the action is still Heaven, but with an ease bred of the timelessness of that realm, the poem has moved from Anne's postmortal heavenly existence to her premortal heavenly existence. This stanza, like the first, is conducted largely in the conditional mode; the possibility that Anne was a poet simply by virtue of inheritance from her father is first proposed, and second is entertained the possibility of a pre-existing soul, formed in the beginning with all other souls, and going a progress through all the great Greek and Latin poets on its way down the ages to embodiment in Anne Killigrew. This latter speculation, involving an identity of soul in a long succession of poets, gives rise to an easy metaphor of Anne as Sappho. The metaphor of Anne as Sappho reincarnate is not mere adornment, not mere idle if graceful compliment, but is of a piece with all the images in the poem that associate Anne with the classical practice or conception of poetry. Indeed, the whole speculation about a pre-existing soul emphasizes a Platonic influence upon Christianity. Tentatively accepting the second speculation, the poet addresses Anne as a *Heav'n-born Mind* and moves into imagery that is possibly biblical; he calls upon Anne's soul to cease its flight on the grounds that there is *no Dross to purge from thy Rich Ore: / Nor can thy Soul a fairer Mansion find.*[8] The last line of the stanza appeals for Anne's return from Heaven to earth: *Return, to fill or mend the Quire, of thy Celestial kind* (1. 38; I, 460K). Taken together with the statement that Anne's soul requires no further mortal purgation, and the statement that her soul cannot find a fairer residence, this line constitutes an appeal to the soul that has informed poets all down the ages to return from Heaven to complete the numbers or repair the harmony of the celestial kind of poets on earth. The second stanza, speculatively and conditionally but nonetheless effectively, is elaborating the metaphor of Anne Killigrew; in the first stanza she was a poetess singing with the seraphim in Heaven, and in this stanza she is the poetic soul that has informed all the great poets. In the first stanza poetry constituted the link between Heaven and earth, between celestial and mortal poet, and in the second stanza poetry is the ground of the appeal to Anne's soul to return. The first stanza is primarily occupied with metaphorizing Anne as participant in celestial harmony; the second stanza extends the metaphorizing by making Anne's soul the vessel of that harmony from before time was, the carrier of that harmony down the ages of history, and the one whose return would restore the full chorus and harmony of the true poets. The metaphorizing does not yet include images of the fall and of atonement—these are withheld until Stanza IV—but from this metaphor of a restoration of full harmony, especially as it appears in the image *mend*, it is an easy step to the Stanza IV terms of a profaned heavenly harmony, a fall and an atonement.

The third stanza gets down to consideration of the birth of Anne. Temporally the progression of the imagery has been from Anne as a soul newly translated into Heaven to Anne as pre-existing soul proceeding through the great poets of history, and now the poem comes to the embodiment of this soul at the birth of Anne Killigrew. The link between Heaven and earth is retained in this stanza because the birth of Anne is considered as an event in both places. Heaven remains dominant here as the locus of most of the imagery. Professor Tillyard has commented on the retention here, as in the first stanza, of the inherited world picture: "Similarly with the stars: he knows about their conjunctions and horoscopes. He uses the technical term *in trine* when he says that the more malicious stars (like Saturn and Mars) were in a benign mood at Anne Killigrew's birth."[9] The stanza continues the gesture of diffidence that has attended all of the metaphorical extension and elaboration of Anne up to this point; *May we presume to say* prefaces the account of the celestial celebration of the birth of Anne. The association of Anne with heavenly harmony is strengthened. *Angels* are her brothers, and at her birth they string their lyres to announce to *all the People of the Skie* that a poetess has been born on earth. The time of her birth was a time most favorable for mortals to hear *the Musick of the Spheres*. The miracle of the bees clustering about the honeyed mouth of Plato has not been renewed for Anne because it was a *vulgar* miracle which Heaven lacked *Leasure* to renew. All the company of Heaven is occupied with

105

solemnizing Anne's birth, and keeping her *Holyday*. She is born, that
is, like a saint, and the day is a holy day *above*. The joy in Heaven
and on earth, the choir of angels, the music of the spheres—all of this
imagery attendant upon the birth of Anne invokes the atmosphere of
the incarnation. The stanza, of course, is in simple fact dealing with
an incarnation, and the imagery serves to make the event like *the* incarnation. The imagery employed by Milton for *the* incarnation in
On the Morning of Christ's Nativity may have had an influential
rôle in Dryden's choice of images:

IX

When such musick sweet
Their hearts and ears did greet,
   As never was by mortall finger strook,
Divinely-warbled voice
Answering the stringed noise,
   As all their souls in blisfull rapture took:
The Air such pleasure loth to lose,
With thousand echo's still prolongs each heav'nly close.

X

.   .   .   .

She [Nature] knew such harmony alone
Could hold all Heav'n and Earth in happier union.

XIII

Ring out ye Crystall sphears,
Once bless our human ears,
   (If ye have power to touch our senses so)
And let your silver chime
Move in melodious time;
   And let the Base of Heav'ns deep Organ blow,
And with your ninefold harmony
Make up full consort to th' Angelike symphony.

(ll. 93-100, 107-08, 125-32)

Whether Milton's imagery attendant upon the nativity actually influenced the images that attend the birth of Anne Killigrew in
Dryden's poem may remain a moot point, but it is certainly worth
remarking that both poets ally the Platonic or Pythagorean music of
the spheres with the song of the heavenly host; in Dryden's ode this
kind of amalgamation of classical and Christian images is an im-

portant and recurrent feature. Furthermore, apart from the question of direct influence, the parallels between Milton's images and Dryden's are close enough to provide strong support for the proposition that Dryden has surrounded Anne Killigrew's birth with imagery appropriate to the nativity of *the* atoning figure. In this way the third stanza completes the metaphorical preparation of Anne Killigrew for the metaphorical service of atonement for a second fall which is imposed upon her in the fourth stanza.

In the fourth stanza, and in all succeeding stanzas except the final one, earth is the main locus of the action and the imagery. Incarnation is the event both of Heaven and earth, but fallen man and the atonement are more completely upon the stage of the world. Atonement is accomplished by the fact of the divine in human form going through an earthly career. The stanzas after the fourth are occupied with Anne's nature on earth and her career as a mortal. The fifth stanza contains a compliment to Anne which, to the modern eye, as Professor Tillyard has observed, may appear inverted:

Such Noble Vigour did her Verse adorn,
That it seem'd borrow'd, where 'twas only born.

(ll. 75-76; I, 462K)

The distance that appears in all cases of borrowing between the borrower and the source does not appear in Anne's poetry. She participates by nature in the noble vigor that adorns past poets, and has no need to borrow. She is born into the birthright of the great classical poets so that there is no need for a movement of acquisition. This way of insisting on the poetic gift that is hers by nature is directly in line with the imagery of the second stanza which insisted upon the identity of the soul of Anne with the soul of the great poets of the past:

It [her soul] did through all the Mighty Poets roul,
Who *Greek* or *Latine* Laurels wore,
And was that *Sappho* last, which once it was before.

(ll. 31-33; I, 460K)

The fifth stanza proceeds to assert in close collocation the integrity of her character and the purity of her muse. One of the images that emphasizes this connection of life and art, of the moral and the

aesthetic, is the metaphor of her father's life as a book in which she
has read. This metaphor is then extended to Anne:

> And to be read her self she need not fear,
> Each Test, and ev'ry Light, her Muse will bear,
> Though *Epictetus* with his Lamp were there.

(ll. 80-82; I, 462K)

As applied to Anne, the image of being *read* refers initially, as in the
case of her father, to her life, but the introduction of *her Muse* carries
the image over to her poetry. The image of the lamp of Epictetus
brought to bear on her life and art is an interesting one in this context. Professor Noyes, in a note on this passage, suggested that
Dryden had confused Epictetus with Diogenes.[10] Professor Kinsley,
in a note on the passage in his edition, also assumed an error on
Dryden's part (IV, 1966K, n. to l. 82). Professor Pierre Legouis,
however, as long ago as 1946, accepted Dryden's reference as accurate and pointed out the probable source in Lucian.[11] It is true
enough that Diogenes' lamp has a luster of familiarity that the lamp
of Epictetus does not have, but since there is, in fact, a lamp traditionally associated with Epictetus, one is bound to consider the
validity of the image of the lamp in connection with that Stoic philosopher. Epictetus had an iron lamp which was stolen, and thereafter
he contented himself with an earthenware lamp. When he died, the
lamp was bought by an antiquarian for three thousand drachmas.
The lamp, apparently, had become a symbol of the wisdom, simplicity of life, and moral integrity of Epictetus. The precepts of this
philosopher present an idealistic morality, an earnest, serious, stern
advocacy of righteousness. He achieved the status of a kind of pagan
saint; his character and teachings were admired by some Christians,
notably Origen, and subsequently efforts have been made from time
to time to prove that Epictetus was influenced by Christianity. His
Manual, with minor changes principally in the proper names, was
adopted by two different Christian ascetics as a rule and guide of
monastic life. The same was done again in the seventeenth century
for the Carthusians by Matthias Mittner (1632), who took the first
35 of his 50 precepts *Ad conservandum animi pacem* from the *Encheiridion*. The lamp of Epictetus, applied to the poetry of Anne
Killigrew, is clearly an image of a stern moral test, and the choice of
Epictetus is particularly nice because classical and Christian are so

108

involved together in this philosopher. As an image, then, Epictetus'
Lamp is another instance of the presentation together of the classical
and the Christian.

Anne's muse has given chaste expression to love. Once again the
connection of art and life is emphasized. *Love* expressed in her poetry
is imaged as a *Lambent-flame* that plays about the breast of the
virgin poetess. She herself is *cold* while her poetry expresses the
Warmth of love; this situation is imaged in classical metaphors:
" 'Twas *Cupid* bathing in *Diana's* Stream" (l. 87; I, 462K). *Diana's
Stream* images the coolness and restraint of the virgin poetess; the
line invokes classical figures to express the restraint exercised by a
Christian poetess. The image of *Diana's Stream* is another way of
saying *Arethusian Stream* and has, of course, the advantage of intro-
ducing the major classical emblem of virginity. Together with the
Christian images of nun, virgin, and atoning figure, these classical
images create the rich content of the general metaphor of Anne
Killigrew.

The imagery of the sixth stanza continues the process of amplifying and explicating the general metaphor of Anne:

> Born to the Spacious Empire of the *Nine,*
> One would have thought, she should have been content
> To manage well that Mighty Government:
> But what can young ambitious Souls confine?
> To the next Realm she stretcht her Sway,
> For *Painture* neer adjoyning lay,
> A plenteous Province, and alluring Prey.
> *A Chamber of Dependences* was fram'd,
> (As Conquerors will never want Pretence,
> When arm'd, to justifie the Offence)
> And the whole Fief, in right of Poetry she claim'd.
> The Country open lay without Defence:
> For Poets frequent In-rodes there had made,
> And perfectly could represent
> The Shape, the Face, with ev'ry Lineament;
> And all the large Demains which the *Dumb-sister* sway'd,
> All bow'd beneath her Government,
> Receiv'd in Triumph wheresoe're she went.
>
> (ll. 88-105; I, 462K)

Professor Tillyard has commented on the political metaphor, the figure of Anne as a ruler and a conqueror, as one of Dryden's "iso-lated" lapses: "It is hard to feel warmly about the political metaphor in stanza six: the idea that through the descriptive passages in her poetry she had staked out claims in the adjacent province of painting, as an ambitious ruler forms seditious groups in the country he means to invade."[12] With respect to this political metaphor, a figure which is introduced at the beginning of this stanza and not dismissed until the end of the following stanza, it is important that the extent to which this metaphor has been prepared for be considered. The idea that Anne has been born into poetry has already been given a double basis, first, in the fact that Anne's father was a poet, and second, in the conceit that the soul embodied in her is the same soul that has informed the great classical poets. This latter conceit particularly has raised Anne to a metaphorical status which can be appropriately described as presiding from birth over *the Spacious Empire of the Nine*. The poetic soul in its past history has in fact presided over the subjects governed by the nine muses. Professor Tillyard, however, does not seem to regard the metaphor as extravagant, as extending the general metaphor of Anne too far, but he is objecting to the metaphor as a special kind of figure, a political metaphor hard to accept in this context. The comparison of a poet to a monarch is one of the most frequent figures in Dryden's prologues and epilogues, as has been seen. It is a thoroughly conventional figure, based on the traditional correspondence between poet and monarch as rulers of their particular realms. It is true that the figure, as used in this stanza, undergoes a bold and rather special development. The figure moves from the emperor presiding over a realm to a conqueror extending his realm. Painting is metaphorized as a province presided over by *the Dumb-sister,* and even the justification of the conquest is metaphorized in political terms. Her reception as a painter is meta-phorized as the triumphant reception of a conqueror.

The operation of Anne's soul as a governing principle in painting is then set forth:

> Her Pencil drew, what e're her Soul design'd,
> And oft the happy Draught surpass'd the Image in her Mind.
> The *Sylvan* Scenes of Herds and Flocks,
> And fruitful Plains and barren Rocks,
> Of shallow Brooks that flow'd so clear,

The Bottom did the Top appear;
Of deeper too and ampler Flouds,
Which as in Mirrors, shew'd the Woods;
Of lofty Trees with Sacred Shades,
And Perspectives of pleasant Glades,
Where Nymphs of brightest Form appear, ⎫
And shaggy Satyrs standing neer, ⎬
Which them at once admire and fear. ⎭
The Ruines too of some Majestick Piece,
Boasting the Pow'r of ancient *Rome* or *Greece*,
Whose Statues, Freezes, Columns broken lie,
And though deface't, the Wonder of the Eie,
What Nature, Art, bold Fiction e're durst frame,
Her forming Hand gave Feature to the Name.
So strange a Concourse ne're was seen before,
But when the peopl'd Ark the whole Creation bore.

(ll. 106-26; I, 462-63K)

She has been imaged as a monarch, and now this new realm of hers is filled in. At the end of the sixth stanza, allusion ascends a step higher, from governing principle to forming principle; the aesthetic world which she governs she also creates. Aesthetic creation is analogized to God's creation. This step reflects the extension, so common in the imagery of the prologues and epilogues, from monarch in a general sense to the archetypal divine monarch.

Professor Tillyard has commented on the lines which present Anne Killigrew's painting: "This is purely descriptive and ornamental. There is not the least sense of any of the things pictured being a part of a cosmic as against a decorative scene. Nymphs and satyrs are simple classical ornament, they are not the classical equivalent of 'real' supernatural beings with their necessary place in the chain. The same is true of the herds and flocks. Nor is there any sense of the landscape being emblematic or of corresponding to any other cosmic plane. Anything that is not purely pictorial is realistic, looking forward to the nature-poetry of Thomson, to the age of science and away from the age of theology."[13]

It is clear that Anne Killigrew's painting is presented in terms of what it includes and what, given its total content, it is like. The images which present what Anne Killigrew's painting includes are the particulars which support the general image already established

111

of her painting as like a province or country and lead to the second general image of Anne's painting as like God's creation. In other words, the imagery here is enriching and extending the general metaphor of Anne Killigrew; the metaphor of Anne has before approached the person of the atonement, and here it approaches the person of the creation.

The particular images of the creation over which Anne Killigrew has presided associate her creation with the original making of the natural world, the imaginative making of classical myths, and the artistic, material making of the monuments of classical Greece and Rome. The fact that in her painting she has represented and re-created these objects is sufficient basis for the image of her painting as like the ark that bore the whole creation. The image also has a basis in the identity established earlier in the poem between Anne's soul and the soul of the great classical authors; Anne as painter represents and *re*-creates what originally her soul created—her soul is *that Sappho last, which once it was before.* She has been imaged as the creative soul born in heaven and persisting through secular time, and this soul represents now in its painting the time-defaced monuments of the classical ideal which it had before shaped and which in its own present activity it continues to embody and to represent *unsoil'd . . . and undefil'd.*

Professor Tillyard's judgment that the "nymphs and satyrs are simple classical ornament" and that there is no "sense of the landscape being emblematic or of corresponding to any other cosmic plane" ignores the apparent effort to present periods and types of creation, *What Nature, Art, bold Fiction e're durst frame,* and to regard artistic creation as allied with and emblematic of divine creation. It is difficult to accept Professor Tillyard's judgment that these lines look "forward to the nature-poetry of Thomson, to the age of science and away from the age of theology" when the image to which they look forward and into which they are received is the image of the ark carrying the epitome of creation. As for the political metaphor, Professor Tillyard may be right that "it is difficult to feel warmly about" it, but the metaphor is designed for thinking in terms of a set of established relations, a set of correspondences and a system of hierarchy in which the values are given. The values and relations are acceptable or unacceptable to the mind; there is no call for powerfully affective images of these relations since the relations in question are neither established nor disestablished by the movement of feeling. To say that "it is hard to feel warmly about" one of the relations in the conventional picture is to say that the picture, for many modern minds, has disintegrated, and the relations that were parts of it no longer touch upon an allegiance of heart and mind to the whole picture; it is to say that the critic is accustomed to the modern situation in which the poet has been dethroned.

The seventh stanza further enlarges the world over which Anne as painter presides by including the contemporary scene as rendered in her portraits of the king and queen:

> The Scene then chang'd, with bold Erected Look
> Our Martial King the sight with Reverence strook:
> For not content t' express his Outward Part,
> Her hand call'd out the Image of his Heart,
> His Warlike Mind, his Soul devoid of Fear,
> His High-designing Thoughts, were figur'd there,
> As when, by Magick, Ghosts are made appear.
>   Our Phenix Queen was portrai'd too so bright,
> Beauty alone could Beauty take so right:
> Her Dress, her Shape, her matchless Grace,
> Were all observ'd, as well as heav'nly Face.
> With such a Peerless Majesty she stands,
> As in that Day she took the Crown from Sacred hands:
> Before a Train of Heroins was seen,
> In *Beauty* foremost, as in Rank, the Queen!
>   Thus nothing to her *Genius* was deny'd,
> But like a Ball of Fire the further thrown,
>   Still with a greater Blaze she shone,
> And her bright Soul broke out on ev'ry side.
> What next she had design'd, Heaven only knows,
> To such Immod'rate Growth her Conquest rose,
> That Fate alone its Progress could oppose.
>
>   (ll. 127-48; I, 463-64K)

The imagery which has established Anne herself as monarch of a realm supports and is supported by the imagery of this stanza. The fact that her portraits represent monarchs not merely in their outward appearance but in their inward essence as well suggests a bond of sympathy between herself and them, a bond which the imagery has already asserted by making Anne herself a monarch. In the case of the portrait of the queen, this bond is broadened to include a shared beauty as well as a shared royalty: *Beauty alone could Beauty take so right.* Her sympathetic observation and understanding extend to the portrayal of the queen's *heav'nly Face.* Her forming hand, her power of design are governed by her *Heav'n-born Mind;* the imagery of the poem has already so defined the origin of her genius, and in this stanza this relationship is reaffirmed and completed by making Heaven alone have knowledge of the end of her creative activity: *What next she had design'd, Heaven only knows.* The hyperbole, however, is not simply downright but skillfully edged by the phrasing with a playful tone. The stanza concludes with the explicit renewal of the metaphor of *Conquest* for Anne's activity as a painter.

In the eighth stanza the general metaphor of Anne Killigrew, which up to this point has been accumulating in the imagery one token after another of earthly and heavenly magnificence, receives emphatic additions of mortality. The effect of these additions, however, is further definition and amplification of the general metaphor of Anne and involves no denial or retraction of what the imagery has worked to establish. This stanza returns to the simple human fact which initiates elegy and strikingly concentrates images of mortality and images belonging to the established celestial aspect of the metaphor of Anne. Anne, *the much lamented Virgin,* lies *in Earth.* Like another mortal poetess, she has succumbed to a disease which disfigured her physical beauty before it killed her. The emphasis of the stanza falls heavily on the flesh and the humiliation of the flesh, the corruption that is the lot of the body. This phase of the metaphor of Anne is important as a corollary of the celestial aspect. The imagery has made her an atoning figure, has stressed her incarnation as such, and the poet has appealed to God to accept her life and work as an atonement. Atonement is accomplished not by sheer divinity, but by a divinity that has assumed a mortal form and, though sinless, suffered the consequences of sin. It is right, then, that the human as well as the divine should appear in the full metaphor of Anne, and in this stanza they are side by side. Anne's death is the plundering and destruction of a *Divine* thing; it is a *double Sacriledge.* The disfiguring of her body is the defacing of a *Shrine* and the taking of her life is the theft of a *Relique*. In the midst of an emphatically mortal dissolution the imagery turns as overtly as ever to characterizing Anne as a divine figure, a saint, and the disease itself is translated by being referred to as the method by which Heaven translates the soul.

In the ninth stanza there are further accents of mortality in the consideration of the effect of her death on earth. Her death is considered as it will affect her brother, who is at sea and on his way home:

> Slack all thy Sailes, and fear to come,
> Alas, thou know'st not, Thou art wreck'd at home!
>
> (ll. 170-71; I, 464K)

Wreck'd at home images the death of Anne as the wreck of her brother's own vessel. The image sharply focuses the destruction of a brother's hope and the desolation of his grief. There is a paradox in having him wrecked where he is not, wrecked in the earthly symbol of the center and source of safety, wrecked in the place toward which he steers. This paradox may derive additional force from the content which has been given to the general metaphor of Anne. Given the full extension of the metaphor of Anne, her wreck is a disaster at the center of things. Her brother on the seas has lost the very goal to which he steered. Implications of this sort seem to be involved in this image, and the imagery of the latter part of the stanza seems to strengthen these implications. The movement, as in the eighth stanza, is from the wrecked Anne to the translated Anne; her brother is bidden to look aloft:

> But look aloft, and if thou ken'st from far,
> Among the *Pleiad's* a New-kindl'd Star,
> If any sparkles, than the rest, more bright,
> 'Tis she that shines in that propitious Light.
>
> (ll. 174-77; I, 464K)

Anne is imaged as a new star among the Pleiades, the constellation which is traditionally associated with the navigation of the seas; the name of the Pleiades is derived from the Greek verb *to sail*.[14] If her death is her brother's wreck at home, her translation is his guide on the seas and a propitious light upon his voyage. She is now no longer an influence and reference point on earth but a guide and

115

influence from above.[15] This imagery of stellification returns the poem to the locus of the imagery with which it began; stellification brings the poem back to the initial speculation about the heavenly seat taken up by Anne. There is a cycle in the positions of the imagery, from a postmortal heavenly existence to a premortal heavenly existence, to incarnation in a succession of earthly poets down the ages of history, to incarnation in Anne, the life of Anne, the death of Anne, and then finally, come full circle, back to the postmortal heavenly state; the cycle involves the progress of a soul, not an individual soul but a great and continuing soul. In the last stanza the cycle and *saecula saeculorum* are done away with the sounding of *the Golden Trump*.

The connection of the imagery used for the birth of Anne with imagery applied to the incarnation has been pointed out by way of Milton's *On the Morning of Christ's Nativity*. There is a similar relationship between Dryden's treatment of the last judgment as the final act of the human drama in which Anne has borne an atoning part, and Milton's treatment of the last judgment as the ultimate fulfillment and completion of the work of atonement to be performed by Christ. Dryden's final stanza begins with these lines:

> When in mid-Aire, the Golden Trump shall sound,
>   To raise the Nations under ground;
>   When in the Valley of *Jehosaphat*,
> The Judging God shall close the Book of Fate;
>   And there the last Assizes keep,
>   For those who Wake, and those who Sleep.
>
> (ll. 178-83; I, 465K)

Milton's Nativity poem has these lines:

> Yet first to those ychain'd in sleep,
> The wakefull trump of doom must thunder through the deep,
>
> .   .   .   .
>
> When at the worlds last session,
> The dreadfull Judge in middle Air shall spread his throne.
>
> (ll. 155-56, 163-64)

The similarities are significant only as they surround the common theme of an atonement; the possibility of direct influence of Milton's ode upon Dryden's is not here in question.

Dryden's last judgment exhibits Anne's fulfillment of her rôle as a redeemer of poets; the action and imagery of atonement which have appeared in the poem are completed here. The character and the action that have been suggested by the imagery more or less strongly in the course of the poem are confirmed in the imagery of this last, climactic scene. *The Golden Trump,* the voice of Heaven which compels all things toward the final ordering and final harmony, will be heard first by the *Sacred Poets.* This conceit has been supported by all the imagery in the poem that represents Anne as a sacred poet participating in celestial harmony—the references to her *Celestial Song* and *Hymns Divine* in the first stanza; the reference, in the second stanza, to *the Quire, of thy Celestial kind;* the references, in the third stanza, to the angelic music attendant upon her birth. All of the imagery of the *Sacred* poet as seen in Anne has established a close bond and sympathy between the sacred poet and the divine voice; the sacred poet cherishes a

> Heav'nly Gift of Poesy

> .   .   .   .

> Whose Harmony was first ordain'd Above
> For Tongues of Angels, and for Hymns of Love.

The singling out of Anne as an atoning figure and all of the imagery attendant upon that process ascribe to Anne a closeness to divinity and the divine voice which is special even among her kind. Accordingly, the last stanza represents Anne as going before and showing the sacred poets the way to Heaven; now she is explicitly addressed as a *Saint*:

> There *Thou,* Sweet Saint, before the Quire shalt go,
> As Harbinger of Heav'n, the Way to show,
> The Way which thou so well hast learn'd below.

> (ll. 193-95; I, 465K)

In this stanza of orthodoxy there is also a covert classical allusion in the lines describing the rising of the poets:

> The Sacred Poets first shall hear the Sound,
>   And formost from the Tomb shall bound:
> For they are cover'd with the lightest Ground.

> (ll. 188-90; I, 465K)

Sit tibi terra levis, the familiar classical epitaph, was very often cut on English tombstones of the period.

Sir Walter Scott remarked of this last stanza: "The last stanza excites ideas perhaps too solemn for poetry; and what is worse, they are couched in poetry too fantastic to be solemn; but the account of the resurrection of the 'sacred poets' is, in the highest degree, elegant and beautiful."[16] Although Scott does not in this case apply the epithet "metaphysical" which occurs so frequently in his editorial comments on Dryden's poetry, it seems probable that his objection is to the yoking together of extremes. *The last Assizes* (like Milton's *last session*) is an image which yokes together the last judgment and the sitting of a British court. This fusion of sacred and secular should be considered in relation to the general method of the imagery by which a secular figure is raised to the status of a saint and metaphorized as a sacred figure performing a sacred function. There are, indeed, some very sharp contrasts in the stanza:

> When ratling Bones together fly,
> From the four Corners of the Skie,
> When Sinews o're the Skeletons are spread,
> Those cloath'd with Flesh, and Life inspires the Dead.
>
> (ll. 184-87; I, 465K)

Dr. Johnson quoted the first two lines of the passage above in support of the remark that Dryden "is sometimes unexpectedly mean." He refers to the image as *intermingled* in the description of "the Last Day, and the decisive tribunal."[17] The image is, indeed, quite as emphatic as anything in Donne's account of the Last Day in the seventh of his Holy Sonnets. The image of *ratling Bones* flying together *from the four Corners of the Skie* is certainly a noisy presence in the general atmosphere of heavenly harmony, the atmosphere determined by the initial *Golden Trump* and the later references to *Quire* of poets singing *like mounting Larkes, to the New Morning*. This is, however, a continuation of the emphatic mortality that attended the saint in the imagery of the eighth stanza. It is the mortality that makes the life and work miraculous and saintly, and it is the mortality, the fact that the very bones shall live, that enhances the final miracle of the divine reordering of elements into harmony. Anne's rôle as an atoning and redemptive poet has been made necessary by the wretched fall of man, made possible by her divine poetic soul and its submission to the suffering and death of the body, and made glorious by participation in the divine harmony which restores

118

mortality even from the extremity of the destruction wrought by sin. *Ratling Bones* are the extreme fact gathered up into the supreme harmony. All through the poem the imagery has worked to create in the general metaphor of Anne Killigrew an emblem of the character and power of that harmony.

Professor Tillyard, some of whose observations on the presence of the inherited, Elizabethan world picture in the poem have already been quoted, concludes these observations with a comment on the last stanza and some general remarks about the poem: "Along with this correctness is the orthodoxy of the last stanza. Anne Killigrew, now in heaven, will reassume her body on the Day of Judgement and reascend to her final heavenly home. It looks as if the old material were there; and yet the emphasis has altered, being now on man and off the rest of creation in a new way. In other words the humanism of the Renaissance, which in Davies was still truly combined with the inherited world picture, has been carried much further and has destroyed the old proportions."[18] With this judgment may be compared Professor Douglas Bush's comments on Dryden's poetry in general: "But the age of Dryden—I am not speaking strictly in terms of chronology—despite obvious outward and some inward marks of continuity with Renaissance culture (as in critical theory), is essentially different. The character of the body of poetry which we have surveyed permits, indeed insists, that the line be drawn between Milton and Dryden. For the substance of Milton's mind is largely a combination of Renaissance humanism and medievalism; there is no such mixture in the writings of Dryden and his fellows. They are classical, after a fashion, but their modes of thought, feeling, and expression have no tincture of the medieval. Thus our outline begins with the most modern of medieval poets, and ends with the most medieval of late Renaissance poets, and in all that lies between Chaucer and Milton we have observed the fusion, complete or incomplete, of the medieval and the classical. . . . While the humanistic and aesthetic values of the classical tradition were united with the religious and ethical force of the Middle Ages, Milton was still possible. . . . Milton is a poet; Dryden is a man of letters."[19]

The judgment of Professor Tillyard in the particular case of this ode is somewhat at variance with the judgment of Professor Bush on

Dryden's poetry in general. Both of these judgments may be considered in relation to such conclusions as may be drawn from the study of the imagery of this particular ode. Professor Tillyard is certainly justified in saying that "it looks as if the old material were there"; "the old material," that is, terms, relations, and structure of the Elizabethan and medieval world picture, is in fact present in this poem and in most of the other poems of Dryden the imagery of which has been examined in previous chapters. It is also apparent that present along with "the old material," the medieval and Christian material, is a different material, the classical material whose presence in combination with the medieval and Christian material can be seen in poets from Chaucer to Milton and has been regarded as one of the hallmarks of the Renaissance. The method and temper of this combination may vary considerably from one author to another and even from one poem to another of the same author. In *On the Morning of Christ's Nativity*, Milton makes a motion of dismissal to the whole throng of "heathen" deities as he celebrates the birth of Christ:

The Oracles are dumm,
No voice or hideous humm
    Runs through the arched roof in words deceiving.
Apollo from his shrine
Can no more divine,
    With hollow shreik the steep of *Delphos* leaving.
No nightly trance, or breathed spell,
Inspire's the pale-ey'd Priest from the prophetic cell.

The lonely mountains o're,
And the resounding shore,
    A voice of weeping heard, and loud lament;
From haunted spring, and dale
Edg'd with poplar pale,
    The parting Genius is with sighing sent,
With flowre-inwov'n tresses torn
The Nimphs in twilight shade of tangled thickets mourn.

                                    (ll. 173-88, pp. 6-7)

It is clear that the gesture of dismissal and even the terms of derogation are partly a skillful poetic feint, because while the heathen deities are being dismissed they are also necessarily being included, and while they are being deprecated they are also being granted power, for the greatness of the power of Christ is being measured partly as it is a strength great enough to drive out the power of the heathen deities. Gestures of dismissal that are similarly ambivalent are familiar in *Paradise Lost*. In *Lycidas,* however, there is no gesture of dismissal, and the deity, without apology, is referred to as Jove. In Dryden's ode there is no gesture of dismissal or utterance of derogation toward the classical material, but rather an elaborate and complicated movement of identification that uses classical for Christian terms just as Milton uses Jove for the supreme being. In the absence of any gesture of dismissal the imagery of Dryden's ode rather suggests an argument of the fundamental likeness of classical moral and aesthetic ideals and the Christian religious ideal. This argument is expressed by taking Anne as a poet, defining her as a classical *and* sacred poet, and by *making* her an atoning figure, metaphorizing her as a saint.

The idea of the sacredness of poets had a classical rather than a Christian origin. Greek drama provided the great example of the alliance of poetry and religion, and there was also the classical tradition of respect and reverence for the inspired utterances of the poet who was regarded as a seer and prophet. There was no parallel biblical conception of the sacredness of the poet, but there were, of course, poetic portions of Scripture. A modern argument such as Sidney's *Defence of Poesy* invoked the classical idea of the poet and appealed to the fact that portions of Scripture were written in poetry, as well as to the consideration that poetry could be a most effective teacher of sacred and specifically Christian truths. This line of argument was developed by Milton in a passage in *The Reason of Church Government*: "But those frequent songs throughout the law and prophets beyond all these, not in their divine argument alone, but in the very critical art of composition may be easily made appear over all the kinds of Lyrick poesy, to be incomparable. These abilities, wheresoever they be found, are the inspired guift of God rarely bestow'd, but yet to some (though most abuse) in every Nation: and are of power beside the office of a pulpit, to inbreed and cherish in a great people the seeds of vertu, and publick civility, to allay the perturbations of the mind, and set the affections in right tune, to celebrate in glorious and lofty Hymns the throne and equipage of Gods Almightinesse, and what he works, and what he suffers to be wrought with high providence in his Church, to sing the victorious agonies of Martyrs and Saints, the deeds and triumphs of just and pious Nations doing valiantly through faith against the enemies of Christ, to deplore the general relapses of Kingdoms and States from justice and Gods true worship. Lastly, whatsoever in religion is holy and sublime, in vertu amiable, or grave, whatsoever hath passion or admiration in all the changes of that which is call'd fortune from without, or the wily sut-tleties and refluxes of mans thoughts from within, all these things with a solid and treatable smoothnesse to paint out and describe. Teaching over the whole book of sanctity and vertu through all the instances of example with such delight to those especially of soft and delicious temper who will not so much as look upon Truth herselfe, unlesse they see her elegantly drest, that whereas the paths of honesty and good life appear now rugged and difficult, though they be indeed easy and pleasant, they would then appear to all men both easy and pleas-ant though they were rugged and difficult indeed."[20] He expressed this idea in his invocation of the "Heavenly Muse" at the beginning of *Paradise Lost,* and there the infusion of the classical muse with a Christian sacredness is very plain. The appeal to the mountains as places where this spirit inhabits is classical; the particular places referred to, however, are Christian:

> Sing Heav'nly Muse, that on the secret top
> Of *Oreb,* or of *Sinai,* didst inspire
> That Shepherd, who first taught the chosen Seed,
> In the Beginning how the Heav'ns and Earth
> Rose out of *Chaos*: or if *Sion* Hill
> Delight thee more, and *Siloa's* Brook that flow'd
> Fast by the Oracle of God; I thence
> Invoke thy aid to my adventrous Song.
>
> (I, ll. 6-13, pp. 181-82)

This idea of a muse informed with a Christian sacred spirit, a Heavenly Muse, is involved in Dryden's representation of Anne Killi-grew as a poetess whose birth was attended by angelic music and who, her *Arethusian Stream* being *unsoil'd* and *undefil'd,* could atone for fallen mortal poets and ultimately lead the redeemed poets up to Heaven. In Dryden's ode, however, there is no suggestion of the *displacement* of the classical informing spirit by the Christian spirit, but rather a suggestion that the two are supplementary or in fact the same, cherishing the same ideals, seeking the same ends. Consequently, the implications of *Vestal* and of *Virgin,* of *Sappho* (and the mighty Greek and Latin poets) and of *Saint, of Arethusian Stream . . . undefil'd* and of atonement are made to revolve about a single figure whose merits can be tested by the Stoic integrity of Epictetus (whose teachings were themselves so readily identifiable with Christianity) as well as approved by the event of the Last Judgment, and amid the medieval and Christian orthodoxy of that final scene the pious wish of classical epitaphs, *Sit tibi terra levis,* is fulfilled to the sacred poets who rise to participate in the final inclusive harmony. The soul of the classical poets and the soul of the saint are one soul; the good poet is the good man.

Some additional light is shed on the method of imaging in Dryden's ode when one compares his method to Donne's method in the *Anniversaries,* noticing first the similarities and then proceeding to the differentiating characteristics. The two methods are fundamentally alike in their treatment of the person whose death is the occasion of the poem. Both Donne and Dryden proceed to use the occasioning person as a base for the erection of a metaphorical structure. Both poets proceed so far with the metaphorical process that the centers of their poems are shifted away from the occasioning person, and Ben Jonson's objection to Donne's poems for Elizabeth Drury might be applied with almost equal justice to Dryden's ode; Dryden, moreover, might quite easily have replied to the objection just as Donne is reported to have replied, that he was presenting the idea of a woman, and not as she was. In support of this view, the roughly parallel case of Dryden's *Eleonora,* "a panegyrical poem," may be mentioned; in this poem Dryden is avowedly following Donne's general method in the *Anniversaries.*

In creating a metaphorical center involving so much more than the mere occasioning personage of the poem, Dryden and Donne can give compliment its full due and avoid any empty flattery; it is sufficient compliment that what is predicated starts from the mere fact, the occasioning person, and the person is secure against flattery because the predicates state an ideal enlargement of the fact to which their burden can be referred. The similarity of method extends also to the lengths to which the basic process is carried by both poets. The imagery of atonement and redemption which Dryden builds around Anne Killigrew can scarcely be regarded as less extreme than Donne's imagery of a central principle of order. The difference between Donne and Dryden is not in the lengths to which they carry their imagery; both go to extremes. The difference appears when one examines how they arrive at these extremes. Donne's poem proceeds disputatively, whereas Dryden's poem proceeds persuasively. Donne cultivates sharp, challenging, astonishing images which provoke surprise or disagreement; his poem is usually engaged in the ingenious justification of images. His images are so striking, so unique, that they require immediate explanation; the situation of perplexity or outright disagreement must be resolved before the poem can proceed. An example of such a situation and the procedure of immediate explanation appears in *A Funeral Elegy* which exhibits a basic conceit of the *Anniversaries*; the poem says, "we may well allow," but we do not allow without the succeeding explanation:

> But 'tis no matter; wee may well allow
> Verse to live so long as the world will now,
> For her death wounded it. The world containes
> Princes for armes, and Counsellors for braines,
> Lawyers for tongues, Divines for hearts, and more,
> The Rich for stomackes, and for backes, the Poore;
> The Officers for hands, Merchants for feet,
> By which, remote and distant Countries meet.
> But those fine spirits which do tune, and set
> This Organ, are those peeces which beget
> Wonder and love; and these were shee; and shee
> Being spent, the world must needs decrepit bee;
> For since death will proceed to triumph still,
> He can finde nothing, after her, to kill,
> Except the world it selfe, so great as shee.

(ll. 19-33)

The first twenty-six lines of *The Second Anniversary, Of the Progress of the Soul* afford another example of this kind of procedure in Donne's poetry; in this case, the metaphor of the *First Anniversary* which makes the death of Elizabeth Drury the world's death must be justified in the poem celebrating the second anniversary of Elizabeth Drury's death. The poem opens by asserting a metaphor that is treated as a main proposition entailing a number of corollaries. In this

case the metaphor is of Elizabeth Drury as the sun, and further as
the Sunnes Sunne; her death accordingly is the setting of the sun.
Since the sun set (Elizabeth Drury died) a year ago and the world
still continues, the world exhibits a kind of everlastingness. A series
of similes is then introduced to demonstrate that the world did actually receive a fatal blow and a termination at the death of Elizabeth
Drury (the setting of the sun), and there are similes and metaphors
within the main similes in a kind of Chinese box arrangement. The
world is, first of all, *as a ship which hath strooke saile* still running
on the force which the sail (Elizabeth Drury) had won to it; the
figure is then shifted directly to *a beheaded man* who still by reflex
movements shows certain signs of life. Within this simile there is the
metaphor of *Red seas* for blood; the metaphor of the soul's flight;
the metaphor of *bed* for heaven; the simile of beckoning to the soul
for the twinkling of the eyes and rolling of the tongue; the simile, for
the reflex movements, of ice crackling at a thaw, thaw being simile
for death; the simile, for the reflex movements, of lute strings crack-
ing in moist weather, with the added touches of *moist* and ringing
her knell enforcing the thing being proved, namely death (the lute
that can ring its own knell—appearance of life, fact of death).
Finally there appears the conclusion:

> So struggles this dead world, now shee is gone;
> For there is motion in corruption.

It has now been demonstrated that, despite motion and signs of life,
the world *is* dead.

There is, then, a great deal of local elaboration and explication
of images in a Donne poem, and consequently there is variety rather
than accord among Donne's images except as they relate to a common center.

Dryden proceeds usually persuasively and by concession. He cultivates agreement. The agreements which he encourages, however,
very often entail consequences somewhat beyond the ostensible pro-
visions of the contract. Consider, for example, the third stanza of
To Anne Killigrew; the stanza begins by asking a gracious permis-
sion:

> May we presume to say, that at thy Birth,
> New joy was sprung in Heav'n, as well as here on Earth.
> (ll. 39-40; I, 460K)

There is nothing very hard about such an agreement. It is not at all like getting agreement to the proposition that, because Elizabeth Drury is dead, the world is dead. Dryden's poem follows up with a triplet in which the word *sure* genially assumes that the presumption has been allowed, but the poem does not immediately presume very far on the agreement:

> For sure the Milder Planets did combine
> On thy Auspicious Horoscope to shine,
> And ev'n the most Malicious were in Trine.

(ll. 41-43; I, 461K)

The lines which follow upon the triplet, however, do, indeed, presume. The poem works the initial concession to its fullest possible value, and if the agreement remains technically unbroken, the imagery certainly gives the agreement the widest possible latitude of interpretation:

> Thy Brother-Angels at thy Birth
> Strung each his Lyre, and tun'd it high,
> That all the People of the Skie
> Might know a Poetess was born on Earth.
> And then if ever, Mortal Ears
> Had heard the Musick of the Spheres!

(ll. 44-49; I, 461K)

The apparently innocuous concession allows the poem to claim a warrant for proceeding to imagery that invokes the atmosphere of the Nativity. *Joy . . . sprung in Heav'n, as well as here on Earth* is referred *ex post facto* to the incarnation. The poem does not insist; the reference of the imagery might perhaps be ignored here, but the poem will return to imagery of this sort. In the next stanza there is the image of the *Fall* followed by the appeal, *Let this thy Vestal, Heav'n, attone for all!* Such imagery does not force the issue,[21] but certainly it does repeat the situation of the preceding stanza, and with the repetition the extensive reference of the imagery is less easy to ignore. The poem goes on suggesting implications of the agreement until, in the final stanza, the suggestion carries more force than previously, but not the force of insistence; in place of imagery *implying* a divine event, as with the Nativity in the third stanza, there is here imagery actually characterizing the divine event of the Last Judgment and presenting Anne Killigrew as an actual figure in that divine event:

126

> There *Thou,* Sweet Saint, before the Quire shalt go,
> As Harbinger of Heav'n, the Way to show,
> The Way which thou so well hast learn'd below.
>
> (ll. 193-95; I, 465K)

Sweet Saint and *Harbinger of Heav'n* showing poets *the Way* are images which touch an accord between Anne and the divine redemptive figure. These images, however, actually affirm no more than the latitude of implication that was suggested as early as the third stanza. The convention that was established, amicably and genially, would be violated in spirit if the poem insisted on the widest latitude. The method is not disputative, and the issue is never raised, but conversely, and as an equal consequence of the convention, the suggestion is never dropped.

The method of persuasion depends upon smooth transitions from one image to another; surprises do not occur very often by the way but only when the ascending movement is all but complete does the elevation attained become evident with some effect of suddenness. It is rather like negotiating a series of windings and turns in the gradual ascent of a hill with the merest glimpses of the view on the way up and then, near the summit, the view widely and on all sides disclosed, yet with limits never quite definable, shapes on the horizon that may be mountains or clouds. It is interesting to notice that some of the most striking images in Dryden's poem occur in the last stanza when they have the justification of a prepared surprise, one that the reader will realize, upon reflection, he has been climbing towards and did in some sort expect. If the features of the view do nevertheless exceed expectation, it should be remarked that the surprise is contained within a traditional scene, and that the treatment of that scene, besides being in accord with Milton's version of it, is, in its imagery, based directly upon the thirty-seventh chapter of Ezekiel and several phrases in the third chapter of Joel. Rattling bones flying together, sinews being spread over skeletons—these are surprising images but they are also the way of casting a traditional scene in traditional terms: "So I prophesied as I was commanded: and as I prophesied, there was a noise, and behold a shaking, and the bones came together, bone to his bone. And when I beheld, lo, the sinews and the flesh came up upon them, and the skin covered them above"

(Ezekiel 37: 7-8). Dryden's one departure from Ezekiel's account is making the bones come together from *the four Corners of the Skie;*[22] it is the breath that inspires the dead that Ezekiel represents as coming from the four winds. Beside such a variation one ought to set the consideration that in invoking the words of Ezekiel for the constitution of his last scene Dryden touches upon a chapter in which are concentrated the traditional prophecy of a restored and reunited nation and the vision of a Messianic figure.

NOTES

1. *To Mr. Oldham* will be used as an abbreviation of the full title, *To the Memory of Mr. Oldham;* and *To Anne Killigrew* will be used for *To the Pious Memory Of the Accomplisht Young Lady Mrs Anne Killigrew, Excellent in the two Sister-Arts of Poësie, and Painting. An Ode.*

2. Since the entire poem appears on a single page (p. 389) in vol. I of Professor Kinsley's edition, subsequent quotations from *To Mr. Oldham* will be identified by line numbers alone.

3. *Aeneid,* VI, l. 866.

4. *Selected Essays* (New York: Harcourt, Brace and Co., [1932] 1947), pp. 273, 274.

5. Renaissance handbooks of classical mythology, and Spenser, for that matter, in allegorizing the distinction between celestial fire and the baser, earthly fire, made Vesta the symbol

of the fire aethereall;

Vulcan, of this, with us so usuall.

(*The Faerie Queene,* VII, vii, 26)

Since Dryden's poem assigns to its central figure a rôle which has social implications, it may be appropriate to recall also that the fire in the temple of Vesta was associated with the health and well-being of the state and that the vestals, besides tending this fire, were the guardians of a sacred pledge upon which the very existence of Rome was thought to depend.

6. *Five Poems, 1470-1870* (New York: Macmillan Co., 1948), p. 60.

7. *Ibid.,* pp. 53-54.

8. See Isaiah 1:25 and John 14:2.

9. *Five Poems,* p. 54.

10. *The Poetical Works of John Dryden,* ed. George R. Noyes (Cambridge ed., Boston, [1909, 1937] 1950), p. 980, n. to l. 82.

11. In a letter to the *Times Literary Supplement,* July 3, 1959, Pierre Legouis called attention to the fact that he had accepted Dryden's reference to Epictetus and cited Lucian as source in the notes to *Dryden Poèmes choisis* (1946). The story of the sale of the lamp appears in Lucian's *The Ignorant Book-Collector,* in *Lucian,* translated by A. M. Harmon (New York, 1921), III, 193: "But why do I talk to you of Orpheus and Neanthus, when even in our own times there was and still is, I think, a man who paid three thousand drachmas for the earthenware lamp of Epictetus the Stoic? He thought, I

suppose, that if he should read by that lamp at night, he would forthwith ac-
quire the wisdom of Epictetus in his dreams and would be just like that
marvelous old man." Professor Samuel H. Monk has indicated to me that he is
adopting the same view of the matter in an American text edition of Dryden.

12. *Five Poems,* p. 50.

13. *Five Poems,* p. 55.

14. There is a possibility, which ought not to go unmentioned, that the
Pleiades are chosen as a constellation congenial to Anne partly because of the
various groups of authors who have borne the name. The invocatory reference
to the Virgin as *stella maris* is perhaps also relevant, and there may be a
recollection of Donne's *First Anniversary,* ll. 223-26:

She whom wise nature had invented then
When she observ'd that every sort of men
Did in their voyage in this worlds Sea stray,
And needed a new compasse for their way.

The Poems of John Donne, ed. Herbert J. C. Grierson (2 vols., Oxford, 1912),
I, 238. All citations of Donne's poetry are from this edition.

15. There is a similarity between this elevation of Anne and that of
Milton's Lycidas:

Now *Lycidas* the Shepherds weep no more;
Hence forth thou art the Genius of the shore,
In thy large recompense, and shalt be good
To all that wander in that perilous flood.

(*Lycidas,* ll. 182-85)

16. *The Works of John Dryden,* ed. Sir Walter Scott, revised and corrected
by George Saintsbury (18 vols., Edinburgh, 1882-93), XI, 104.

17. *Lives of the Poets,* ed. G. B. Hill (3 vols., Oxford, 1905), I, 463.

18. *Five Poems,* p. 54.

19. *Mythology and the Renaissance Tradition in English Poetry* (Min-
neapolis, 1932), pp. 294, 297.

20. Preface to the Second Book, *The Works of John Milton,* ed. F. A.
Patterson (18 vols., New York, 1931-38), Vol. III, Part I, pp. 238-39.

21. This reticence becomes usual Augustan practice. Professor Maynard
Mack has described Pope's development of a variety of reticent modes of
imaging—" 'Wit and Poetry and Pope': Some Observations on His Imagery,"
Pope and His Contemporaries (Oxford, 1949), pp. 20-40.

22. Dryden's language here seems clearly designed to recall the picture
of the judgment day scene drawn by Donne in the seventh of his *Holy Sonnets*:

At the round earths imagin'd corners, blow
Your trumpets, Angells, and arise, arise
From death, you numberlesse infinities
Of soules, and to your scattred bodies goe.

(*Holy Sonnet VII,* ll. 1-4)

Various John Dryden

RYDEN WAS, in a way, all his life a victim of occasions, public occasions in terms of which he cast up much of his poetic account. The last decade of his life was a public occasion too in its coincidence with the last decade of his century. In the 1690's many of the turbulent conflicts of the extraordinarily troubled century had been worn out by their own violence and wearied into a sort of peace; at the same time various John Dryden had sailed into his own port and could look back on the stormy seas he had traversed. Repeatedly in the prefaces and poems of this decade Dryden expresses himself as looking back, reviewing, summing up, imbued with the attitude of a captain at the end of a voyage. The personal attitude gains in symbolic resonance by its congruence with the end of the century.

The last turn in the infinite variety of Cleopatra was marble constancy, a turn which both completed and converted the cycle of her variousness. Some such paradox of variety and constancy applies in the case of Dryden and has bedeviled his critics; it is his fatal charm. In *The Hind and the Panther* he wrote:

> My thoughtless youth was wing'd with vain desires,
> My manhood, long misled by wandring fires,
> Follow'd false lights; and when their glimps was gone,
> My pride struck out new sparkles of her own.
> Such was I, such by nature still I am.

> (Part I, ll. 72-76; II, 472K)

He had, in the judgment of some, lackeyed the varying tide until he rotted himself with motion. Even in his final Roman choice he could be accused of timeserving, but his Roman choice survived the Roman king, a king whose actions Dryden did not much approve. Under William, the Protestant king, Dryden, as translator of the *Aeneid,* could be expected to dedicate the epic poem to the reigning monarch, but this time Dryden, very likely to the despair of his publisher, Tonson, would not dedicate to the king. Dryden had lost his official positions as poet laureate and historiographer royal, and the income that was important to a man at his age, and he was losing his health, yet never in his long career did he undertake so much or write so serenely well. If he had all his life courted favor, and favored courts, he seems to have been at his best last, when out of favor. He bravely showed the way toward authorship supported without patronage. To Dryden, in the last decade of his life, the king was nothing. He was, at the end of his career, more willing than ever before to leave the world to Caesar; he saw more clearly that Caesar was beguiled. The Hind had advised "a long farwell to worldly fame":

> And what thou didst, and do'st so dearly prize,
> That fame, that darling fame, make that thy sacrifice.
>
> (Part III, ll. 289-90; II, 511K)

There may be a quibble in the word *worldly,* but Dryden did, at any rate, in important ways, sacrifice his worldly fame. Possibly there remained *that darling fame* which he, no more than Milton, could give up.

Dryden's imagery throughout his poetry discloses very much evidence of almost unremitting preoccupation with the problem of authority. In praise and blame, in panegyric and satire, and in the modulated poems of discursive, reasonable argument, the heart of the matter is authority, a quest for the countenance that compels the term *master.* A characteristic tension, a partial failure and a peculiar success in Dryden's poetry, are produced by the persistent effort to locate authority *in* the world. The drama of this attempt centered upon the image of the king while the historical drama of the royal symbol moved in the other direction; Albert Camus, speaking of the end of this historical drama in France, summarized its significance in this way: ". . . the fact remains that, by its consequences, the condemnation of the King is at the crux of our contemporary history. It symbolizes the secularization of our history and the disincarnation of the Christian God. Up to now God played a part in history through the medium of the kings. But His representative in his-

tory has been killed, for there is no longer a king. Therefore there is
nothing but a semblance of God, relegated to the heaven of principles."[1]* It may well be that Dryden's effort was, in Santayana's
phrase, a belated masquerade. Since Dryden's age was in the process
of transmuting the king into "an idol monarch, which their hands
had made," the king image and its ambiguity threatened to change
and dissolve on Dryden's hands. So far as Dryden's late verse is concerned, the secular monarch seems almost to have resigned his part
in what is "immortal and unchang'd."

The poetry of Dryden's last decade is filled with memorable
images expressive of an enlarged sense of the world and a reduced
sense of the world's importance; the images are vivid, firm, compre-
hensive, and judicial:

> Theirs was the Gyant Race, before the Flood.
> The second Temple was not like the first.
> > (*To . . . Mr. Congreve*, l. 5 and l. 14; II, 852K)

> *All, all, of a piece throughout;*
> *Thy Chase had a Beast in View;*
> *Thy Wars brought nothing about;*
> *Thy Lovers were all untrue.*
> > (*The Secular Masque*, ll. 92-95; IV, 1765K)

Dryden had contended for wit against dullness, for stability against
the whirl of fashion, for reason above passion, for the poet-maker
against the facile imitator, for learning against obscurantism, for the
true fire against random enthusiasm, for political authority above
popular whim. In all of these contentions he had appealed to and for
the image of the king. In his last poems he has not abandoned—he
could not abandon—his habitual images, but the scale of meaning
has altered under the influence of his new total perspective. There is
a world that he has been disburdened of, a public world. The political
sanction or pseudo sanction of his laureateship has been lifted from
his shoulders and he holds the office of poet unofficially—unofficially
but perhaps religiously, the sacredness without the solemnity. In the
Prologue to *Love Triumphant* (late 1693 or early 1694) Dryden
presents himself in the image of one resigning the symbols of office.
In his new freedom he practises a set of pieties toward a fellow poet

Notes for this chapter are on page 147.

and dramatist, toward a gracious lady, and toward a kinsman and namesake. His finest powers are shown in these poems, without straining, genially and surely.

Two poems of this last decade are the finest examples of Dryden's mastery of a middle style; they are the epistles *To my Dear Friend Mr. Congreve, On His Comedy, call'd The Double-Dealer* and *To my Honour'd Kinsman, John Driden, of Chesterton.* The former illustrates very well the special virtues of a style that means not colorless compromise but a balanced prospect of conversational informality and dignified elevation. The middle style reigns by a smooth alternation and intermingling, by laying under contribution both lords and commons in language and imagery. The tone restricts and smiles at the dignity imported by imagery. Consider the manner of the beginning in this epistle:

> Well then; the promis'd hour is come at last;
> The present Age of Wit obscures the past.

(ll. 1-2; II, 852K)

The language of this couplet puts forward suggestions full of dignity and elevation; the moment of the fulfillment of prophecy is, after long expectation, at hand, and its coming marks a significant revolution of time. It is midway in the second line that *wit* is established as the subject under discussion. Thus the aura of suggestion is, in one continuous motion, powerfully developed and cleanly restricted; the falcon is flown and then called, a fiction is indulged and then modified. If the fiction were offered only to be withdrawn, the proceeding would be as barren as a magician's trick in which an offered object vanishes in a convenient sleeve. There is, however, true wit in the stylistic maneuver because the fiction leaves its impress upon the statement, the solemn suggestions have been made smilingly, and their true seriousness will emerge in the course of the poem. The wit, in fact, is in the beginning; *Well then,* says the speaker, as preface to the solemn statement, a sort of small type for the second coming. *Well then,* says the speaker, implying that the solemnity that follows is the enforced consequence of something that has gone before. The something that has gone before is Congreve's play, and with the advent of such wit, who can but prophesy? The prophet is a little reluctant, surprised by fulfillment, ironic at his own expense. The prophet sees himself ousted as he welcomes one greater than the

133

prophets—*Well then*. . . . It is in this matrix that the solemnities of the couplet are to be entertained.

With such an attitude a great deal of dignity can be supported, as this poem proceeds to prove. As the triumph of the new age is proclaimed, a perspective is achieved on the past age and a summary view of history presented. The Elizabethans are "the Gyant Race, before the Flood." The Restoration writers tamed and cultivated the sheer strength of wit that they inherited, but the process of refinement and polishing sapped the original strength:

> Our Builders were, with want of Genius, curst;
> The second Temple was not like the first.
>
> (ll. 13-14; II, 852K)

Thus Dryden continues to write the history of wit with the dignity of biblical history and symbols. Wit has had its period when there were giants in the earth, has had its obliterating flood, has had its peerless temple destroyed and has built a second temple that is no match for the first. And now wit has, in Congreve, its architect of genius whom Dryden dignifies with Roman honors:

> Till You, the best *Vitruvius*, come at length;
> Our Beauties equal; but excel our strength.
>
> (ll. 15-16; II, 852K)

But the prophetic background to the symbolic temple building also points to the founder and builder in the biblical tradition, the Messiah whose pronouncement about destroying and building the temple was so bold and so misunderstood.

Possibly the temple-building image as Dryden carries it out is actually threefold in its suggestions:

> Firm *Dorique* Pillars found Your solid Base:
> The Fair *Corinthian* Crowns the higher Space;
> Thus all below is Strength, and all above is Grace.
>
> (ll. 17-19; II, 852K)

Besides the naming of Vitruvius, the Roman architect, and the tacit suggestion of the Messianic temple builder, the style of the building might suggest to Dryden's audience some features of the style of St. Paul's restored by Sir Christopher Wren after the London fire of 1666. As though conscious of the heavy load thus laid on, Dryden expands to a triplet and concludes with an Alexandrine. He is no mean temple builder himself, and he knows how to found grace in strength. Moreover, he is for the moment done with the expansive structures which imagery can build, and the triplet and Alexandrine have the effect of summarizing and concluding a movement rehearsed in the terms which the opening lines so smilingly and ironically licensed.

Having explored, on the one hand, within significantly qualifying limits the dignity and elevation that are within the grasp of the middle style, the poem turns directly to a nearly prosaic statement of Congreve's qualities and literary lineage so that formal dignity is quickly counterbalanced by simplicity of diction:

In easie Dialogue is Fletcher's Praise.

(l. 20; II, 852K)

For ten lines the poem moves in an easy, flowing, conversational style, and the symbolic figure of the temple with its strength and grace is done over in nonfigurative simplicity in a summarizing enumeration of qualities of strength and grace found in Etherege and Southerne and Wycherley and combined in Congreve's work. This prosaic summation, like the earlier figurative one, rests on a triplet with final Alexandrine.

The first major section of the poem (the first "paragraph" of forty lines) concludes with a renewed Roman and Renaissance allusiveness in which the drama of the speaker's relationship to Congreve, so brilliantly hinted in the opening line, is more explicitly presented. Essentially it is the drama of the old master and the bright and shadowing surprise of young genius; the poem mixes dignified allusion with informal directness, honoring the young man with names like Scipio and Raphael, and qualifying with a word like *beardless*. The colors of the picture are so mixed that virtue appears on both sides, in the young man whose grace attracts consent and in the older man who graciously offers his homage and submission. Tensions and animosities latent in the situation are recognized and overcome.

The second major section of the poem begins with a significant change in tone, and the imagery that is employed alters the aspect of the situation. Heretofore the speaker has spoken collectively of himself and his age as though they were at one in their attitudes and recognitions, as though the age were as ready as he to recognize the

new master in the kingdom of wit. The shadow of actuality now falls
upon the prophet and forerunner, and Dryden's archetypal image
of his age, the image of the king deposed, appears:

> Oh that your Brows my Lawrel had sustain'd,
> Well had I been Depos'd, if You had reign'd!
> The Father had descended for the Son;
> For only You are lineal to the Throne.
> Thus when the State one *Edward* did depose;
> A Greater *Edward* in his room arose.
>
> (ll. 41-46; II, 853K)

In this drama the speaker and Congreve are at one, king and prince,
father and son, their tensions dissolved in relationship; now the tension of conflict is between them and the actually reigning powers of
the age. As poets, both are victims of a usurpation:

> But now, not I, but Poetry is curs'd;
> For *Tom* the Second reigns like *Tom* the first.
>
> (ll. 47-48; II, 853K)

The speaker's tone ranges from lament to indignation. He confronts
facts, he denounces, but then he lifts his eyes to the future and prophe-
sies with renewed confidence. The accent of the language employed
at the beginning of the poem returns with its overtones of solemnity,
but qualified by wit, an enacting and mimetic wit in the versification,
the signature of the speaker's and Congreve's legitimate claim to the
throne:

> Yet this I Prophesy; Thou shalt be seen,
> (Tho' with some short Parenthesis between:)
> High on the Throne of Wit; and seated there,
> Not mine (that's little) but thy Lawrel wear.
>
> (ll. 51-54; II, 853K)

The first parenthetic expression here is the formal equivalent of the
stated meaning. This witty consorting together, this quick dancing
movement in which form and content visibly strike hands, characterizes the conclusion of this second section which renews the
affirmation of Congreve's genius:

> So bold, yet so judiciously you dare,
> That Your least Praise, is to be Regular.
>
> (ll. 57-58; II, 853K)

136

Regularity is the least praise of such a couplet. Unevenness of stress and boldness of rhyme enact the qualities described. In the next couplet the statement is of genius exceeding the measure of what can be laboriously learned or taught, and the couplet exceeds the measure with an Alexandrine. The next three lines are the third crescendo in the poem's praise of Congreve, the third summation of his powers, and they match the others, they are a formal return, as the verse expands to a triplet and concludes with an Alexandrine:

> To *Shakespeare* gave as much; she cou'd not give him more.
>
> (l. 63; II, 853K)

The verse extends itself to its farthest reach; it cannot give more.

The final verse paragraph moves to a new aspect of the speaker's relationship to Congreve; the speaker appeals to Congreve to be the guardian and preserver of his fame. A final development in the imaged character of both the speaker and Congreve occurs in this last act of the poem's drama of their relationship. The appeal casts Congreve in a rôle like that of savior, a diminished form of that rôle because the speaker's seriousness goes beyond the fiction to "Heav'n" and "Providence," and also in the rôle of strong, young hero in battle and in the plain simplicity of the part of friend. The speaker appears as prophet, as king, as abdicating playwright, as man worn with age, as vanquished warrior, and as friend. Most of these rôles have appeared before, so that the last paragraph resumes established motifs; they are all brought together to be resolved in a concluding harmony, and rather than the motifs themselves, it is this harmony that remains to be described. Both persons of the drama have, in the last act, two general modes of existence; these two modes are perhaps most clearly developed as they apply to the suppliant speaker. First, there is his existence as man, and second, his existence as name, the former the thin-spun life to be slit by the abhorred shears of the blind Fury, but the second to be preserved, the life beyond life, the surviving fame. On the one hand, the speaker bequeaths nothing; he is poor and in debt. On the other hand, he is rich with honors and bequeaths his laurels to his descendant. His poverty is the care of providence:

> Unprofitably kept at Heav'ns expence,
> I live a Rent-charge on his Providence.
>
> (ll. 68-69; II, 853K)

His wealth of fame is a hero's care:

Let not the Insulting Foe my Fame pursue;
But shade those Lawrels which descend to You.

(ll. 74-75; II, 854K)

Very generally these two modes may be designated as Christian and classical; the speaker exists as an aged prophet, a Simeon, a dying sinner, and as a vanquished hero, and Congreve as a good man, and as a surviving hero. The blending of these two notions animates all of the language. The departure of man-victim and artist-hero doubles the significance of "th' Ungrateful Stage." The blending produces such a fine result as the doubled reverberation in *the Insulting Foe*. Surely *the Insulting Foe* is *Tom the First* and *Tom the Second* and all their tom-cat progeny to the last literary generation. Dullness, however, is the *Dunciad* counterfeit of death. The language of this passage holds also the deeper suggestion that death is *the Insulting Foe* who crumbles the body and must be kept from dominion over the fame.

The most important achievement in this poem is brought about by skillful control of tone. Tone, of course, voices the various stages in the movement of the poem's dramatic action, but in this poem the tones gradually sharpen the image of the speaker, causing the *persona* of the elder poet to emerge and distinctly play its part. That part has its own strategy of movement from the opening irony to the final moving appeal. The wryness of the opening compliment, the speaker's suggested disadvantage, his gradual rise to the throne on which he seats Congreve, his bestowal of his laurels upon the younger man, his claim of obligation exerted upon his friend and heir—this sequence of tones constitutes the skillful and reticent drama of the older poet's retained pride, a drama which enhances the integrity of the tribute to Congreve. Dryden's development and strategic employment of a *persona* as a culminating effect of tone look forward to Pope's great successes in the use of masks in his satiric poems.[2]

The judgment of Scott, Van Doren, and other critics that Dryden was an improving poet to the last would certainly have pleased Dryden, because he thought so himself. He was, in the poem to Congreve, the artful master of a *persona* representing the old poet, and this artful mastery appears more directly as self-mastery in the letters and prefatory comments which are related to his last volume called *Fables,* published in March of 1700. He managed to deprecate himself and the ills of old age with a fine irony while retaining the image of pride in his latest achievements; in February of 1699 he wrote to his relative, Mrs. Steward: "In the mean time, betwixt my intervalls of physique and other remedies which I am useing for my gravell, I am still drudging on: always a Poet, and never a good one. I pass my time sometimes with Ovid, and sometimes with our old English poet, Chaucer; translating such stories as best please my fancy; and intend besides them to add somewhat of my own: so that it is not impossible, but ere the summer be pass'd, I may come down to you with a volume in my hand, like a dog out of the water, with a duck in his mouth."[3] In November of 1699, in another letter to Mrs. Steward, Dryden is clearly pleased that the Earl of Dorset and Charles Montague, having seen two poems to be included in the *Fables* volume, one to the Duchess of Ormond and the other to his cousin, John Driden, are of the opinion that he has never written better. In his Preface to the *Fables* Dryden expresses his own judgment of the state of his abilities in the work of this last volume: "I think my self as vigorous as ever in the Faculties of my Soul, excepting only my Memory, which is not impair'd to any great degree. . . . What Judgment I had, increases rather than diminishes; and Thoughts, such as they are, come crowding in so fast upon me, that my only Difficulty is to chuse or to reject; to run them into Verse, or to give them the other Harmony of Prose. I have so long studied and practis'd both, that they are grown into a Habit, and become familiar to me" (IV, 1446-47K). The poem to the Duchess of Ormond provides an example of what these latest developments, especially the still increasing judgment, mean when applied to the poem of compliment, and it is fortunate that in this poem we have a late instance of Dryden at work in the extended and soaring kind of compliment.

The first thing to be said about the imagery of this poem is that we have encountered most of it before; it has become habitual with Dryden, and a detailed study of its materials would be repetitious. What does seem desirable is the more difficult attempt to describe the qualities of this imagery as it is here managed and to find appropriate terms to designate and define the facility of manner that this poem achieves. It seems to me that in this poem Dryden has done something special to cast all of the imagery in high relief. Along with the occasion of compliment he has made imagery itself, and the poetic process of imaging, an overt subject of his poem. The result is that images are not simply presented but are subjected to a philosophical consideration as they appear; the process of imaging is being scrutinized as the images are put forward. As the full title of the poem suggests, Dryden's topic here is not simply the Duchess of Ormond and what can be made of her as an object of compliment, but it is the presentation of a poem to one who is herself the subject of poetry, and what we get is a poetic consideration of the relations between the subject matter of poetry and the poem, the center and the concentric circles of poetic statement at varying radial distances, the thing itself and what may be poetically predicated of it. Dryden performs an act of praise, an act that he has performed over and over in the course of his career as a poet, but this time, as part of his general concern to sum up and review, he gives an added dimension to his poem; this dimension is achieved by a luminous displayed consciousness of what it is like and what it means to write poetry.

Dryden begins with a bold tribute to Chaucer, a tribute that sets Chaucer in the company of Homer and Virgil. The accommodation in time is really double because Chaucer is praised in a couplet which suggests very well the whole characteristic activity of English classicism:

The Bard who first adorn'd our Native Tongue
Tun'd to his *British* Lyre this ancient Song.

(ll. 1-2; IV, 1463K)

Dryden himself undertakes, in succeeding lines, to tune an ancient compliment to his modern purposes; Juvenal had written that Virgil's poetry put Homer's palm in doubt, and Dryden now adapts the remark to Chaucer's entrance into the company of the masters. Here we have a handsome instance of the readiness and even eagerness with which English classicism at its best could accept great figures of the native tradition and award them rank with the greatest figures in its literary pantheon. Dryden's judgment of Chaucer is an early example of the splendid flexibility which put the stamp of classic upon Milton's epic and accepted Milton as the equal and even the superior of Homer and Virgil. At its best English classicism is alert to discern through veils of style and place and time the classic form.

140

Dryden's poem conveys the timeless equivalence of the great poets in language that is not of one poet or one time but an easy composition of ancient and modern. Homer, Virgil, and Chaucer are ranged together around central themes which they have all undertaken, and the circle from past to present is completed with the inclusion of Dryden who is entering upon a subject dealt with by Chaucer before him. Dryden proceeds to argue and to explain this equivalence, working up to his images by hypothesis and a sequence of logic, a method adapted and modified from the metaphysical poets; as Dryden employs the method, the argument leads to the images rather than following them, in the manner of Donne, as justification of an initial shock and elaborated demonstration of the validity of an opening surprise. Dryden's premise here is Platonic—that Chaucer and he, working from different instances, have both been creating from the same idea of beauty—and he caps the argument with the Platonic myth of cyclical return of all things to their original conditions and relationships. The poets stand on the same plane, always and everywhere, and their subjects are the same. These general propositions seem, in turn, to govern the handling of imagery in this poem, images being the various poetic predications, the subject in its imaginative diversity; the outlines of a particular theory and method of imagery have been implied once the fundamental oneness of the major poetic subjects is asserted. The proper image is not the unique or merely original image, but the image which, however new in itself or new by infusion from a new context, continues the link with the past and brings the past to bear in the present. Thus the voices of great poets may continue to speak.

It should be observed that besides drawing the thread of time into a circle from which the major poets face a common center, the first section of Dryden's poem entertains the idea that the occasions of poetry are at times equivalent; it is suggested that the line of creative development leading from a noblewoman of the fourteenth century to the character of Emily in Chaucer's *Knight's Tale* may be entered upon again by a seventeenth-century poet who, beginning with a woman in many ways analogous to Chaucer's original, arrives at the same character. To the poetic imagination two points of actuality may entail the same idea and lead to the same character realized in a work of art. There is a dancing continuity of movement between the actual and the ideal, between the subject and the poetic images of the subject which the poem emphasizes by a series of free transpositions asserting the indifference of names:

> O true *Plantagenet,* O Race Divine,
> (For Beauty still is fatal to the Line,)
> Had *Chaucer* liv'd that Angel-Face to view,
> Sure he had drawn his *Emily* from You:
> Or had You liv'd, to judge the doubtful Right,
> Your Noble *Palamon* had been the Knight:
> And Conqu'ring *Theseus* from his Side had sent
> Your Gen'rous Lord, to guide the *Theban* Government.
>   Time shall accomplish that; and I shall see
> A *Palamon* in Him, in You an *Emily.*
>
> (ll. 30-39; IV, 1464K)

Chaucer draws the character of Emily from the Duchess of Ormond; the Duke and Duchess of Ormond become Palamon and Emily and in their lives enact the poem. All change; all remain. In the words of Yeats, "All things remain in God," and:

> Birth is heaped on birth
> That such cannonade
> May thunder time away,
> Birth-hour and death-hour meet,
> Or, as great sages say,
> Men dance on deathless feet.[4]

Thus far Dryden's poem has circled its center with the primary purpose of establishing the recurrence of Chaucerian subject and Chaucerian poetic result. From this point on, however, other circles of predication are drawn around the poetic center and the initial suggestion of the affinity of major poets and major poetic themes is amply illustrated. The poem moves around its center in paths of imagery widened into highways by the greatest movements of poetry. The Chaucerian images are not lost but continued and extended; the recurrence is not only with Chaucer and his *Knight's Tale* but also with Virgil's and Homer's epics, with Virgil's *Pollio,* and with the Old and New Testaments, creation, paradise, flood, and second coming. The simplicity of the act of making a poem to the Duchess of Ormond becomes, in the luminous consciousness of this poem, the recurrent and manifold act of poetry, and the single subject radiates light through a whole universe of poetic images. The poem has many ways of saying this, but the universality is most clearly asserted in astronomical imagery; Ormond and Emily, at the center, are repeatedly compared to the sun, and Dryden's use of this imagery is a recurrence, with a difference, of Chaucer's imagery.[5] The Platonic myth sets forth in astronomical terms the theme of universal recurrence:

> As when the Stars, in their Etherial Race,
> At length have roll'd around the Liquid Space,
> At certain Periods they resume their Place,
> From the same Point of Heav'n their Course advance,
> And move in Measures of their former Dance.
>
> (ll. 21-25; IV, 1464K)

We are prepared, then, for the full sweep of the poem's orbit, prepared for recurrences that lie along the orbit, prepared for inclusiveness and reminiscence in the method of the imagery.

The two principal circuits of imagery are classical and biblical, and as circles drawn about a common center, the analogy of these poetic predications is implied. The first cycle of classical imagery is drawn from epic, primarily from Virgil's *Aeneid,* and it presents a miniature of the full epic voyage:

> Already have the Fates your Path prepar'd,
> And sure Presage your future Sway declar'd:
> When Westward, like the Sun, you took your Way,
> And from benighted *Britain* bore the Day,
> Blue *Triton* gave the Signal from the Shore,
> The ready *Nereids* heard, and swam before
> To smooth the Seas; a soft *Etesian* Gale
> But just inspir'd, and gently swell'd the Sail;
> *Portunus* took his Turn, whose ample Hand
> Heav'd up the lighten'd Keel, and sunk the Sand,
> And steer'd the sacred Vessel safe to Land.
>
> (ll. 40-50; IV, 1464K)

Within this image of the epic voyage, with its suggestion of the full cycle of the movement from Troy to Italy, from the darkened past to the bright future, Dryden's poem includes the daily cycle of the sun's voyage through the heavens, and along with the pronounced epic features, there is, possibly, a glancing reminiscence of Desdemona's passage to Cyprus, the guiltless keel subduing the elements, beauty as a sacred symbol of harmony, an ordering principle. The poem takes advantage of the fact that, as governors, the Ormonds have once voyaged to Ireland, and the voyage that is "presaged" repeats a previous voyage; the future is a prepared path leading into the past, a new movement renewing an old cycle.

Virgil's epic of government served for the image of the first voyage to Ireland, and Virgil's *Pollio,* the eclogue of prophecy, is the image of the voyage to come:

> When at Your second Coming You appear,
> (For I foretell that Millenary Year)
> The sharpen'd Share shall vex the Soil no more,
> But Earth unbidden shall produce her Store:
> The Land shall laugh, the circling Ocean smile,
> And Heav'ns Indulgence bless the Holy Isle.
>
> Heav'n from all Ages has reserv'd for You
> That happy Clyme, which Venom never knew;
> Or if it had been there, Your Eyes alone
> Have Pow'r to chase all Poyson, but their own.[6]
>
> (ll. 80-89; IV, 1465K)

Tradition saw in the *Pollio* a mystical occurrence of Christian prophecy in a classical context, and Dryden's poem takes complete advantage of this parallelism of Christian and classical predication, fortifying the suggestion with a clear biblical signature (*Your second Coming*) in the opening line. Speaking with the tongues of classical tradition and Christian revelation, of Virgil and the prophets, Dryden's poem says anew what has been said before. There is no competition or discord, only concentration upon the one statement, coincidence of images in one predication. The ordering of experience is a recurrent poetic problem, and the major cycles of experience are always like and unlike the cycles that have preceded. The second voyage repeats the first and each in turn repeats the great voyages of experience and prophecy that poetry has recorded and imagined. Language and imagery, Dryden shows us, can be used to uphold and preserve the continuity of experience. This is the way to be greatly original, not original narrowly in terms of self, but largely original, making the sources of poetry flow in the present. The present subject of poetry is the old subject:

From the same Point of Heav'n their Course advance,
And move in Measures of their former Dance.

Poetic ordering of experience as conceived in this poem is congruent with universal order. The Duchess figures in the order and movement of the heavens, the macrocosm in which she is like the sun. She figures also as microcosm, the faultless frame of the four governed elements, and the cycle from disorder to restoration which has been run in social terms, in terms of Ireland and of mankind, can be run in individual terms, in terms of sickness and restoration to health. The imagery of this process, however, makes us look from end to end of the order, from macrocosm to microcosm, while we examine disease in the individual. First there are the macrocosmic images:

Rest here a while, Your Lustre to restore,
That they may see You as You shone before:
For yet, th'Eclipse not wholly past, You wade
Thro' some Remains, and Dimness of a Shade.

(ll. 103-06; IV, 1466K)

Then there is the disease imaged in the microcosm:

Now past the Danger, let the Learn'd begin
Th'Enquiry, where Disease could enter in;
How those malignant Atoms forc'd their Way,
What in the faultless Frame they found to make their Prey?
Where ev'ry Element was weigh'd so well,
That Heav'n alone, who mix'd the Mass, could tell
Which of the Four Ingredients could rebel;
And where, imprison'd in so sweet a Cage,
A Soul might well be pleas'd to pass an Age.

(ll. 111-19; IV, 1466K)

The poem not only makes us see the problem of order at a number of different levels by a series of concentric movements, circling the universe of divine creation, but also enacts for us the parallel problems of poetic order. This double process is continuous through the whole poem and sharply present in this passage where overt consideration of the problems of creativity, the elements and the faultless frame, merges the activities of God and the poet. One poetic voice after another speaks in the couplet that images God-perfected creation of man:

145

And where, imprison'd in so sweet a Cage,
A Soul might well be pleas'd to pass an Age.

The poets, too, have labored to perfect their sweet cage.

The conclusion of Dryden's poem praises the restoration of all
order in the restored health of the Duchess; by this act, Heaven renews the life and ordered movement of all conditions of men, including the condition of poet:

> Bless'd be the Pow'r which has at once restor'd
> The Hopes of lost Succession to Your Lord,
> Joy to the first, and last of each Degree,
> Vertue to Courts, and what I long'd to see,
> To You the Graces, and the Muse to me.
>
> (ll. 146-50; IV, 1467K)

The completion of the cycle of the poem returns to the beginning and
renews the initial expression of the poem's central symbol as seen by
Chaucer, Virgil, and Homer. From *The Knight's Tale* comes the
imagery of red and white, Mars and Venus, ordered in Theseus'
banner as here in the warlike Duke of Ormond and his fair consort,
together, and individually in the symbolic Duchess:

> O Daughter of the Rose, whose Cheeks unite
> The diff'ring Titles of the Red and White.
>
> (ll. 151-52; IV, 1467K)

The Duchess renews virtues of Homer's Penelope:

> All is Your Lord's alone; ev'n absent, He
> Employs the Care of Chast *Penelope.*
>
> (ll. 157-58; IV, 1467K)

And of Virgil's Dido:

> For him Your curious Needle paints the Flow'rs:
> Such Works of Old Imperial Dames were taught;
> Such for *Ascanius,* fair *Elisa* wrought.
>
> (ll. 160-62; IV, 1467K)

The major predications in the imagery of the poem return in this
passage with marvelously concentrated force and expression; the
Duchess is, first and last, the sun and the stars in their courses. The
lights of day and night are smoothly evoked from Chaucer's imagery
and presented in a couplet that suggests the cycle of a day:

Who Heav'ns alternate Beauty well display,
The Blush of Morning, and the Milky Way.

(ll. 153-54; IV, 1467K)

A blend of Milton and metaphysical boldness resumes the biblical imagery that has gone into the creation of the symbol:

Whose Face is Paradise, but fenc'd from Sin:
For God in either Eye has plac'd a Cherubin.

(ll. 155-56; IV, 1467K)

With the summation of these cycles of imagery reminiscent of all the ways in which the poem has presented the cycles of experience and suggesting the perfection of the completed circle, a point of rest, the poem faces the future and suggests the renewal of the past as the new generation moves on the metaled ways of past and future:

All other Parts of Pious Duty done,
You owe Your *Ormond* nothing but a Son:
To fill in future Times his Father's Place,
And wear the Garter of his Mother's Race.

(ll. 165-68; IV, 1467K)

The *pietas* which recognizes obligations to past and future and manages to resolve and harmonize these duties in the present is a classical ideal; it provides the method of Dryden's imagery. This ideal governs Dryden's practice as a poet, and this poem is a signature of that ideal, one of its triumphs.

NOTES

1. *The Rebel,* trans. Anthony Bower (New York, 1956), p. 120.

2. See the discussion of the Prologue to *All For Love* (pp. 44-46 above), an earlier example of superbly controlled tone and the extension of tone in a *persona.*

3. *The Letters of John Dryden,* ed. Charles E. Ward (Durham, N. C., 1942), p. 109.

4. *The Collected Poems of William Butler Yeats* (New York, 1947), "Mohini Chatterjee," pp. 284-85.

5. E. g., "Up rose the sun, and up rose Emilye," etc.

6. Parallel lines in Dryden's translation of the *Pollio* are:
Unlabour'd Harvests shall the Fields adorn.

(l. 33; II, 888K)

No Plow shall hurt the Glebe, no Pruning-hook the Vine.

(l. 50; II, 888K)

The Serpents Brood shall die: the sacred ground
Shall Weeds and pois'nous Plants refuse to bear.

(ll. 28-29; II, 888K)

Epilogue

GREAT DEAL OF Dryden's poetry is public in character. Dryden frequently addressed himself to the contemporary situation, to public behavior and public events, and very often on public occasions. His poetry repeatedly faced up to the difficult demands of *speaking* to many and speaking *once,* and did so in a situation that was full of change, controversy, and confusion. Donne had lamented the passing of old agreements; Dryden confronted the resultant turmoil. The results which Donne so impressively saw as caused events—"Shee, shee is dead, shee's dead" —were now themselves causes, shaping or unshaping the course of events. Prince to subject was not only a relationship forgotten, but the deposition and execution of a king had illustrated the abandonment. Not only was the element of fire quite put out, but Hobbes' philosophy, denying immaterial substance, threatened to put out soul and God. The old model was gone and a new model had been tried in its place, for the Puritans were busily interpreting Christian revelation not as offering the pattern of monarchy but as supporting a system of commonwealth, though they were unable to agree among themselves as to the exact features of that system. The setting aside of traditional interpretation in favor of private inspiration led to a plurality rather than a unity of political ideas. The Deists urged setting aside not only the traditional, authoritative interpretation of Christian revelation, but the revelation itself, and advocated reliance on Reason and the order of nature to teach men the nature of God and the proper ordering of human society. Locke argued the adequacy of human understanding to the ordering of society. Hobbes

advanced upon the confusion with the secular and desperate remedy of a monolithic state.

Dryden, however, while he experienced political revolution and an attempted new order early in his life, and experienced throughout his life a continuing revolution in thought and belief, experienced also a political restoration of the monarch and a modified renewal of the old order. The breach, as Dryden came to realize, had had grave, irrevocable effects; Charles II could not, on his return, occupy the position of his royal predecessors because there were now too many who regarded the king as a convenience, and of their own fabrication, *An Idoll Monarch which their hands had made.* Yet the restoration itself was a wonder. Evelyn termed the year of the event "Annus Mirabilis," and, though himself an ardent supporter of the king, found the event quite beyond hope: "29 [May] This day came in his Majestie *Charles* the 2d to London after a sad, & long Exile, and Calamitous Suffering both of the King & Church: being 17 yeares: This was also his Birthday, and with a Triumph of above 20000 horse & foote, brandishing their swords and shouting with unexpressable joy: The wayes straw'd with flowers, the bells ringing, the streetes hung with Tapissry, fountaines running with wine: The Major, Aldermen, all the Companies in their liveries, Chaines of Gold, banners; Lords & nobles, Cloth of Silver, gold & vellvet every body clad in, the windos & balconies all set with Ladys, Trumpets, Musick, & myriads of people flocking. . . . I stood in the strand, & beheld it, & blessed God: And all this without one drop of bloud, & by that very army, which rebell'd against him: but it was the Lords doing, *et mirabile in oculis nostris*: for such a Restauration was never seene in the mention of any history, antient or modern, since the returne of the *Babylonian* Captivity, nor so joyfull a day, & so bright, ever seene in this nation: this hapning when to expect or effect it, was past all humane policy." There were also grimmer scenes, harsh acts of justice, symbolic acts by which the monarchy sought to erase a stain: "17 [October] This day were executed those murderous Traytors at Charing-Crosse, in sight of the place where they put to death their natural Prince, & in the Presence of the King his sonn, whom they also sought to kill: taken in the trap they laied for others: The Traytors executed were *Scot, Scroope, Cook, Jones.* I saw not their execution, but met their quarters mangld & cutt & reaking as they were brought from the Gallows in baskets on the hurdle: ô miraculous providence of God." Evelyn had for a while the pleasure of recording signs of a general return to things as they were: "25 [November] Dr. Rainbow preach'd *coram Rege* on 2. Luk: 14. of the Glory to be given God for all his mercys, especialy for restoring the Church, & government: & now was perform'd the service with Musique, Voices &c, as formerly."[1]*

As late as 1666 Dryden could offer a vision of the king and the city together, united by the bond of common suffering (the fire of London); in an address dedicating *Annus Mirabilis* to "the Metropolis of Great Britain," Dryden wrote: "You have come together a pair of matchless Lovers, through many difficulties; He, through a long Exile, various traverses of Fortune, and the interposition of many Rivals, who violently ravish'd and with-held You from Him: And certainly you have had your share in sufferings." He could see in the city "as far as Humanity can approach, a great Emblem of the suffering Deity" (I, 48, 49C; I, 43K) and city and king related to a common pattern of suffering and restoration. The burning of London could be a refining fire. He speaks in the same passage of the city as a Phoenix; a deeply meaningful regeneration could provide a context that would extend and enhance the significance of the physical restoration of the city and the political restoration of the king.

Yet the voices of those who had attempted and supported another order were only briefly quiescent. They read the fire as a different and partial divine judgment, and soon made the fire itself the subject of charges and countercharges, memorialized eventually in the solid dubiety of a column whose inscription charged the Catholics with responsibility for the fire.[2] Opposition to the king soon renewed its strength and subjected Charles II to a growing series of hampering encumbrances and indignities. The idleness of Charles himself (which Dryden punned on in calling him *an Idoll Monarch*) became a source of embarrassment and concern to many of his supporters (including Evelyn). When, in 1681, Dryden's *Absalom and Achitophel* appeared, the earlier vision of people and monarch allied in a common course of suffering and regeneration was replaced by a new picture of division between people and monarch. The emblem of suffering Deity was focused upon the king, and the people of

Notes for the Epilogue are on page 167.

London were represented as causes of, rather than participants in, his suffering. The poem ended with a restoration, but a restoration represented as the reassertion of the sterner aspects of the monarch—those aspects related to the power, law, and judgment of the Deity—enforcing renewed dutifulness from his subjects:

> He said. Th' Almighty, nodding, gave Consent;
> And Peals of Thunder shook the Firmament.
> Henceforth a Series of new time began,
> The mighty Years in long Procession ran:
> Once more the Godlike *David* was Restor'd,
> And willing Nations knew their Lawfull Lord.
>
> (ll. 1026-31; I, 243K)

This is no longer the coming together of *matchless Lovers* but rather of a stern father and a wayward son. Yet this limited kind of restoration, though it does not express an ideal harmony, continues the emblematic habit of seeing relationships within the social order against a macrocosmic background of man's relationship to God. If the people could not be seen as the New Testament's sons of God, they were in any case the Old Testament's children of God. And Dryden held tenaciously to the general metaphor of a restoration; he persistently related the return of social harmony to the return of man into a harmonious relationship with God, and though confronted with recurrent failures of the former restoration, he saw these present failures as occurring within a framework of ultimate divine success.

In the prologues and epilogues where Dryden made a detailed examination of the London scene and presented the picture of a fallen world, he was anatomizing a broad, spreading social failure. In conducting his analysis, he was employing and sharpening the instrument of a relatively new versification, but it should also be observed that he was continuing a kind of examination practiced by Donne, and continuing it to some extent in terms of categories and relations and even images that belonged to a medieval and traditional picture of the world. The following prologue, several passages of which have been discussed heretofore in various particular connections, will serve adequately to illustrate the mode of these continuations:

151

If yet there be a few that take delight ⎫
In that which reasonable Men should write; ⎬
To them Alone we Dedicate this Night. ⎭
The Rest may satisfie their curious Itch
With City Gazets or some Factious Speech,
Or what-ere Libel for the Publick Good,
Stirs up the Shrove-tide Crew to Fire and Blood!
Remove your Benches you Apostate Pit,
And take Above, twelve penny-worth of Wit;
Go back to your dear Dancing on the Rope,
Or see what's worse the Devil and the Pope!
The Plays that take on our Corrupted Stage,
Methinks resemble the distracted Age;
Noise, Madness, all unreasonable Things,
That strike at Sense, as Rebels do at Kings!
The stile of Forty One our Poets write,
And you are grown to judge like Forty Eight.
Such Censures our mistaking Audience make,
That 'tis almost grown Scandalous to Take!
They talk of Feavours that infect the Brains,
But Non-sence is the new Disease that reigns.
Weak Stomacks with a long Disease opprest,
Cannot the Cordials of strong Wit digest:
Therfore thin Nourishment of Farce ye choose,
Decoctions of a Barly-water Muse:
A Meal of Tragedy wou'd make ye Sick,
Unless it were a very tender Chick.
Some Scenes in Sippets wou'd be worth our time,
Those wou'd go down; some Love that's poach'd in Rime;
If these shou'd fail————
We must lie down, and after all our cost,
Keep Holy-day, like Water-men in Frost,
Whil'st you turn Players on the Worlds great Stage,
And Act your selves the Farce of your own Age.

(P, *Loyal General,* ll. 1-34; I, 163-64C; I, 205-06K)

Noisy, distracted, unreasonable, mad, factious, rebellious, corrupted, apostate—the assemblage of terms realizes a whole series of disruptions of relationships, and presents the loss of coherence in gradations of seriousness and in different kinds, ranging from the mere interruption of attention and sequence to the interruption of logical connection to the disease of the connective power itself, and from the breaking of the relationship of subject to prince to the breaking of relationship to God. Yet the imagery which creates this picture of chaos also plays through the portrait suggestions and reminiscences of order. The several disruptions are presented as like one another, as related: madness and unreason striking at sense are like rebels striking at kings; the style of poets who write badly rebels against the authority of good style as the English in 1641 rebelled against the king, and the mistaking critics of poetry judge badly as did the English of 1648 who condemned Charles I; the distracted age is mirrored on a corrupted stage—twice in this prologue life and literature, the period and its drama, are rhymed; the audience that will not attend to good plays is *apostate;* nonsense does not merely prevail but takes the monarch's place and reigns; the whole scene is a *Shrovetide* scene, a festival of misrule, with all sorts of apprentices taking the law into their own hands. The traditional correspondences appear as outcroppings in the various analogies, and the traditional medieval metaphor of the body politic, itself an interrelation of orders, individual to social, a microcosm to a macrocosm, is employed at length in presenting nonsense as a disease which has taken the place of reason —the health, and proper monarch, of the individual and of society. The prologue suggests, by its series of interrelations, both a central monarchal cause and a continuous line of connection between the apparently trivial and the thoroughly serious, between folly and vice, between noise and rebellion, between nonsense and apostasy. This is close to, though not quite, the Donne picture; a surprising number of the parts are here, and a surprising number of the relations, but in place of the metaphor of the decease of Elizabeth Drury is the metaphor of a new and false monarch misruling, and the metaphor of disease, meaning chaos and meaning death. Prologues of this kind look forward, like *Mac Flecknoe,* to the reign of the monarch Dulness in Pope's *Dunciad,* but they are also a sharp and later realization of Donne's perception of a world that is "crumbled out againe to his Atomies."

The survival, in Dryden's poetry, of relationships and metaphors that were traditional not only for Donne but for the Elizabethans is

by no means confined to the prologues and epilogues. Professor Tillyard finds the first stanza of Dryden's *A Song for St. Cecilia's Day,
1687* the "best known rendering in English poetry, keeping strictly to
the old tradition,"[3] of the metaphor of creation as an act of music:

> From Harmony, from heav'nly Harmony
>   This universal Frame began.
>   When Nature underneath a heap
>   Of jarring Atomes lay,
>   And cou'd not heave her Head,
> The tuneful Voice was heard from high,
>   Arise ye more than dead.
> Then cold, and hot, and moist, and dry,
> In order to their stations leap,
>   And MUSICK'S pow'r obey.
> From Harmony, from heav'nly Harmony
>   This universal Frame began:
>   From Harmony to Harmony
> Through all the compass of the Notes it ran,
> The Diapason closing full in Man.
>
> (ll. 1-15; II, 538K)

At the conclusion of his preface to *Absalom and Achitophel* (1681)
Dryden, though aware of the current of the time, suggests the relevance of the old relationship of the individual order to the social
order: *"If the Body Politique have any Analogy to the Natural, in my
weak judgment, an Act of* Oblivion *were as necessary in a Hot, Dis-
temper'd State, as an* Opiate *woud be in a Raging Fever"* (I, 216K).
In the poem itself the body politic metaphor underlies the references
to disturbances in the state as disease:

> This Plot, which fail'd for want of common Sense,
> Had yet a deep and dangerous Consequence:
> For, as when raging Fevers boyl the Blood,
> The standing Lake soon floats into a Flood;
> And every hostile Humour, which before
> Slept quiet in its Channels, bubbles o'r:
> So, several Factions from this first Ferment,
> Work up to Foam, and threat the Government.
>
> .   .   .   .
>
> The Tampering World is subject to this Curse,

To Physick their Disease into a worse.

.　　.　　.　　.　　.　　.　　.　　.

These Ills they saw, and as their Duty bound,
They shew'd the King the danger of the Wound:
That no Concessions from the Throne woud please,
But Lenitives fomented the Disease.
                    (ll. 134-41, 809-10, 923-26; I, 220, 237-38, 240K)

In *Absalom and Achitophel,* as in Shakespeare's *Henry IV,* the sun image is applied to the king and the rebellious forces are represented as governed by the moon.

These survivals of an older picture of the world in Dryden's poetry have sometimes been overlooked in critical statements about Dryden and his relationship to "medievalism"; Professor Bush, for example, would terminate medievalism in Milton,[4] but it will not do to put a period to medievalism with Milton simply because its survival to that point is already an embarrassment to expectation. One must face with as much equanimity as possible the task of describing still later forms of its appearance. A useful description of the differences between Dryden and Milton needs to describe the fashion of Dryden's medievalism as well as of his classicism.

The correspondence of the king to God, the *roi soleil* image that was an Elizabethan commonplace, and the metaphor of the body politic represent survivals of the medieval framework as it applied to the state and the ruler of the state and to the relationship of the individual to society. It is, after all, not so very surprising that, in this area, Dryden's royalism remains closer than Milton's republicanism to traditional correspondences and metaphors. The survival of these elements in Dryden is closer to some aspects of Donne's medievalism than to Milton's, and this closeness seems to stem from their common concern for a principle of authority and the monarchal metaphor, the *eikon basilike*. It must be recognized, of course, that in Dryden's prologues and epilogues the elements of the old tradition appear in a rewoven tapestry, looking themselves more old than new but looking out upon a new scene in which they are involved with new developments. There is the uncongenial and centrifugal development of the city reflected in the London prologues and, countering this development, the new expression of traditional centripetal forces in the metaphor of Oxford. London and Oxford

155

appear in the tapestry as new metaphors, the former negatively and the latter positively related to the old order. These new metaphors, though they emerge directly from the contemporary scene, become powerful as value signs by being brought into contact with elements of the tapestry which have traditionally designated value and disvalue; the two traditions which provide these value designations are the Christian and the classical.

Dryden, like other English poets, finds the classical tradition useful and important because of its difference from and its relevance to the Christian tradition and the modern world. The most assiduous Renaissance allegorizing of classical myth never obliterated the difference, and the Puritan denunciation of pagan myth and the heathen world never quite obscured the relevance. This represents, of course, broadly speaking, the situation in all analogy, since perfect likeness is not analogy but identity. The classical tradition is, in fact, not simply relevant *and* different but relevant *because* different. The classical analogies of English poetry are informed in varying degrees with the sense of difference and the sense of relevance. In *Paradise Lost,* where the subject is theological, some explicit assertion of difference is regularly conveyed along with the classical comparisons. In *Lycidas,* on the other hand, the Deity is referred to as Jove without overt expression of difference; "the Pilot of the *Galilean* lake" and "the dear might of him that walk'd the waves" are also present, distinct but not dissevered from the classical atmosphere because of the central equivocation of the poem. Dr. Johnson's conceptions of relevance and difference were outraged by the poem: "Among the flocks and copses and flowers appear the heathen deities, Jove and Phoebus, Neptune and Aeolus, with a long train of mythological imagery. . . . With these trifling fictions are mingled the most awful and sacred truths, such as ought never to be polluted with such irreverent combinations. The shepherd . . . is now a feeder of sheep, and afterwards an ecclesiastical pastor, a superintendent of a Christian flock. Such equivocations are always unskilful; but here they are indecent, and at least approach to impiety, of which, however, I believe the writer not to have been conscious."[5] The most notable inflammations of the sense of difference occur in the never quite closed gap between Christian theology and classical mythology. No such intense flare-ups threaten the unparted ligature between the classical and the modern world; an easy, strong, assured sense of relevance characterizes the analogies of classical history to modern history.

The classical tradition meant for Dryden many of the same things that it meant for Milton—it provided genres, it shaped style, it enlarged or pervaded content. In the matter of content, however, it meant for Milton, because of his subjects, mythology, whereas for Dryden, because of his subjects, it more often meant history. Its relevance and difference, as employed by Dryden, were more often the relevance and difference of an actual though nonetheless symbolic world. In Milton's narrative classical material appeared frequently in the form of episode adumbrated (as in the well-known Eve-Proserpina analogy) or presented in some detail, sometimes as analogy founded on a relatively narrow base of contact, entered by a gate of association and explored, frequently with the discovery of unexpected richness of relation even in apparently peripheral details (as in the analogy of Mulciber's fall). Milton imported a host of fables, carefully so labeled in *Paradise Lost,* deprecated by the poem as truth but needed as *corpus;* they provided an imaginative extension in which the straitness of sacred truth and sacred myth limbed out and positively flourished. In combination with Christian myth they created areas where meaning acquired the richest texture. Dryden's classical analogies are, in contrast, not only often historical rather than mythological, but also more structural than textural, or if textural, becoming so as the result of quite a different method. Dryden's classical analogies seldom bulk large, are seldom developed at length, but his frequent sprinkled analogic allusiveness does nonetheless leaven the texture of the whole.

Analogic use of the classical tradition as history is rare in Milton's poetry. There are a few examples in the sonnets and a few in *Paradise Lost.*[6] In Milton's prose, however, one finds the kind of classical analogy that is so frequent in Dryden's prologues and epilogues. In *John Milton's Defense of the English People against Claude Saumaise's Defense of the King,* for example, Milton, accusing Charles I of the poisoning of his father, likens him to Nero and in the *Second Defense* supports his proposals for a permanent ruling council by reference to the examples of the Areopagus of the Athenians and the Senate of Rome. It is this kind of reference that is so usual in Dryden's

poetry. The transit from English to Graeco-Roman history is frequent and casual, so casual, indeed, that one needs to remind one-
self that there is, for Dryden as there was for Milton, an awareness
of difference as well as of relevance with respect to the classical tradi-
tion. When Dryden considers classical mythology in the context of a
proposed Christian epic, one is reminded of the deprecatory tags in
Paradise Lost: " 'Tis Objected by a great *French* Critique . . .
Boileau, that the Machines of our Christian Religion in Heroique
Poetry, are much more feeble to Support that weight than those of
Heathenism. Their Doctrine, grounded as it was on Ridiculous
Fables, was yet the Belief of the Two Victorious Monarchies, the
Grecian, and the *Roman*."⁷ Similarly, in *Religio Laici*, where Chris-
tian faith is the subject, the discussion of revelation leads to a state-
ment of the deficiency of Reason as an instrument of religious insight
even in the *Gyant Wits* among the *Heathens*:

> Hence all thy *Natural Worship* takes the *Source*:
> 'Tis *Revelation* what thou thinkst *Discourse*.
> Else, how com'st *Thou* to see these truths so clear,
> Which so obscure to *Heathens* did appear?
> Not *Plato* these, nor *Aristotle* found:
> Nor He whose Wisedom *Oracles* renown'd.
> Hast thou a Wit so deep, or so sublime,
> Or canst thou lower dive, or higher climb?
> Canst *Thou*, by *Reason*, more of *God-head* know
> Than *Plutarch, Seneca*, or *Cicero*?
> Those Gyant Wits, in happyer Ages born,
> (When *Arms*, and *Arts* did *Greece* and *Rome* adorn)
> Knew no such *Systeme*: no such Piles cou'd raise
> Of *Natural Worship*, built on *Pray'r* and *Praise*,
> *To One sole* GOD.
> Nor did Remorse, to Expiate Sin, prescribe:
> But slew their fellow Creatures for a Bribe:
> The guiltless *Victim* groan'd for their Offence;
> And *Cruelty*, and *Blood* was *Penitence*.

(ll. 70-88; I, 313K)

But when Dryden is not considering the management of a Christian
epic or matters of faith and revelation, the difference and relevance of
the classical tradition appear in quite another way. This mode of difference is perhaps best represented by the epigraph affixed by Dryden

to his translation of Virgil: *"Sequiturque Patrem non passibus Aequis"* (II, 867K). The difference is as prominent as the suggestion of filial intimacy. Emulation and kinship, emulation and a sense of distance, perspectives of awe and attitudes of veneration characterized Dryden's relationship to Virgil and to epic poetry: "A Heroick Poem, truly such, is undoubtedly the greatest Work which the Soul of Man is capable to perform" (III, 1003K). Of Virgil's representation of Aeneas Dryden wrote: "Where a Character of perfect Virtue is set before us . . . there the whole Heroe is to be imitated. This is the *Aeneas* of our Author: this is that Idea of perfection in an Epick Poem, which Painters and Statuaries have only in their minds; and which no hands are able to express. These are the Beauties of a God in a Humane Body" (III, 1006K). The sense of distance included for Dryden a feeling of disparity between the English and Latin languages as literary instruments, and the sense of relevance led to extensive borrowing of Latin words, Latin turns of phrase, and a general attempt to accommodate English to Latin: "I Trade both with the Living and the Dead, for the enrichment of our Native Language. We have enough in *England* to supply our necessity; but if we will have things of Magnificence and Splendour, we must get them by Commerce. Poetry requires Ornament, and that is not to be had from our Old *Teuton* Monosyllables; therefore if I find any Elegant Word in a Classick Author, I propose it to be Naturaliz'd, by using it my self: and if the Publick approves of it, the Bill passes" (III, 1059K). As Virgil had been guided by Homer and had used the Trojans to shape a Roman ideal, so Dryden was disposed to use classical authors and eminent Greek and Roman figures at large in the shaping of an English ideal.

The classical tradition meant for Dryden a whole, complete world; it did not mean—and here he is like Milton and all the English poets before him—a religion or a theological framework. It meant a world with certain eminent places—Athens, Sparta, Thebes, Rome—distinguished by a full and completed history out of which they had emerged with several and distinct values so that they could now be used to evaluate a new and current history:

What *Greece,* when Learning flourish'd, onely Knew,
(*Athenian* Judges,) you this day Renew.
(P, Oxford, 1673, ll. 1-2; I, 146C; I, 369K)

Our Poets hither for Adoption come,
As Nations su'd to be made Free of *Rome;*

.   .   .   .

Thebes did His Green, unknowing Youth ingage,
He chuses *Athens* in His Riper Age.

> (P, *Oxford, 1676,* ll. 29-30, 37-38; I, 156C; I, 376K)

It meant a world with certain eminent men whose names, and the
rôles they played, survived their particular history and attained the
status of symbols; they could be used to formulate a history that was
still forming:

As *Cato* did his *Affricque* Fruits display:
So we before your Eies their *Indies* lay:
All Loyal *English* will like him conclude,
Let *Caesar* Live, and *Carthage* be subdu'd.

> (E, *Amboyna,* ll. 19-22; I, 152K)

You who each day can Theatres behold,
Like *Nero's* Palace, shining all with Gold.

> (P, *Opening the New House,* ll. 5-6; I, 148-49C; I, 378K)

Then *Sophocles* with *Socrates* did sit,
Supreme in Wisdom one, and one in Wit.

> (P, *Oedipus,* ll. 3-4; I, 167K)

It meant a world that had its own gods and heroes, and a literature
already submitted to the thorough sifting of time:

But to the little Hectors of the Pit
Our Poet's sturdy, and will not submit.

> (P, *Secret-Love,* ll. 22-23; I, 107K)

So cold herself, whilst she such Warmth exprest,
'Twas *Cupid* bathing in *Diana's* Stream.

> (*To Anne Killigrew,* ll. 86-87; I, 462K)

But when to Praise from you they would Aspire
Though they like Eagles Mount, your *Jove* is Higher.

> (P, *Oxford, 1674,* ll. 36-37; I, 152C; I, 373K)

Converse so chast, and so strict Vertue shown,
As might *Apollo* with the Muses own.

> (E, *Oxford, 1674,* ll. 29-30; I, 153C; I, 374K)

All together it meant a world that had declined and fallen and had survived its ruin, leaving monuments broken, but to the eye of the imagination whole, whole as symbols and models, available to admiration:

> The Ruines too of some Majestick Piece,
> Boasting the Pow'r of ancient *Rome* or *Greece,*
> Whose Statues, Freezes, Columns broken lie,
> And though deface't, the Wonder of the Eie.
> (To Anne Killigrew, ll. 119-22; I, 463K)

In considering the use to which Dryden's poetry puts its major sources of imagery, one needs to focus attention upon the several kinds of material in Dryden's poetry. The social character of much of Dryden's poetry, and of Augustan poetry in general, poses in a special way the problem of translating what is local and particular into what is general. No one is surprised that in nineteenth-century poetry there is a problem of whether the private sensibility of a poet can be made adequately public, and whether highly individualized representation can be shared with an audience, but there is a superficial paradox in the discovery that a society's customs and the public persons and events of an age may be private; Augustan poetry, with its ideal of general Nature *semper et ubique,* undertook to generalize a society and the public kind of event. The corporate experience of a place and of an age had to be translated into the general experience of mankind; the problem involved turning history into narrative and persons into characters. One finds Dryden confronting a special Augustan form of the problem in most of the poems examined in this study. Where the subject is man in society, and where the foreground is occupied with actual details of social experience, as in the prologues and epilogues and in *Absalom and Achitophel,* the simplest form of generalization by the use of imagery is historical analogy comparing a single person or episode in contemporary English history to a person or episode in classical or biblical history. Many instances of this method have already been cited. The historical allegory or parallel is an extension of this method to include a number of persons and a series of episodes; the obvious example is *Absalom and Achitophel.* Such an extended metaphor has the effect, as has been argued in the discussion of that poem, of producing an action that is at one remove from the specific details of both histories. Another method is the occasional suggestion or persistent adumbration, by way of nonhistorical imagery, whether epic or theological, of a formulated narrative or dramatic action; this method is also illustrated in *Absalom and Achitophel*. This third method is important because it formulates, organizes, and evaluates history in a way that isolated historical analogy or even extended historical parallel cannot. The third method actually suggests a narrative structure for history and, in doing so, makes sequences of actual events manageable by extending a number of the events into, or anchoring some of them in, an aesthetic and value order. The application of these methods, and especially of the third method, generalizes history and distills essential value situations. Much of the effectiveness of the attack upon the Puritans, for example, is obtained by making the assault bear upon a kind of disvalue of which the Puritans are merely local symptoms, and the strength of the king appears not in Charles, nor even to any great extent in David, but in the God imagery that cloaks the king as a symbol. Within this framework can be mounted a brilliantly effective, far-reaching assault on all who with their mouths say "Lord, Lord" while their hearts are with Mammon and their hands in the greasy till, and on all who would bring out from under the counter a conception of society as a mere aggregation of interests. The imagery of God and anti-God holds history in a value context where pious phrases wrapped around economic immorality become a frightening blasphemy, and where the absurd facsimile of the good social order shaped around the image of "economic man" becomes an apostasy.

Besides these three methods of generalizing persons and events (three forms in which classical and Christian reference appears), there is another mode of generalization which Dryden's poetry employs and which, in quite a different way, floats a large body of contemporary detail. This method, quite simply, begins with general principles; it is a method of the discursive poem or verse epistle, and *Religio Laici* is the convenient example. The foreground of this kind of poem is, in the beginning, general; the trick is to keep it so, yet without neglecting the local form of issues and principles. In the case of the methods previously discussed, the movement is from the particular to the general by way of analogy and extended parallel and adumbrated narrative, and the terms employed in the movement are agents and actions having the degree of concretion supplied by history or epic or theological drama. In the case of *Religio Laici,* history gives texture and concrete illustration to an argument; the general principles of reason and divine revelation and the question of worship in its public aspect dominate the poem. A modern reader is likely to feel that there is not enough tension between particularity and general principles in this poem, and to overlook the fact that there is, in this kind of discourse on religious practice, a peculiar danger of sinking into a morass of merely contemporary issues, and a special difficulty in keeping hold of the concerns of mankind. The very skillful generalizing of the issues of the argument is supported by the *persona* of the reasonable man recognizing and responding to the voices of reasonable men in all ages, saving Socrates in spite of Athanasius, establishing a continuity of moderation. The poem immediately opens out broad reaches of history back of the issues of the moment, and makes the generalization more powerful by associating the major principles of the argument with the traditional age-old imagery of light.

Turning away from poems in which Dryden faces the problem of the particular and the general in characteristic Augustan forms, one may see the problem in a form familiar to all writers of elegies and odes in *To Mr. Oldham* and *To Anne Killigrew.* In place of society or a set of principles, the base in these poems is a person, and the way of generalization, in these forms, has been trodden by many poets before and since Dryden. It is Dryden's way of managing the generalization that bears the Augustan hallmark. In *To Mr. Oldham* the generalization is by way of classical imagery (both the *semper et ubique* natural images and the specific allusions); in *To Anne Killigrew* the generalization is by way of classical and Christian imagery together. And in both poems there is the generalizing influence of conventional form.

To Mr. Oldham is perhaps the best example of what Dryden can do *within* the classical tradition. This poem handles the themes of a young man's death and a poet's fame, and treats them without touching the ark of sacred reference. The poem attains its maximum extension within the limits of nature, the theme of fame, and the curb of fate; it is half a *Lycidas,* designed to complete its circuit in classical terms. It does not agitate a moral problem or religious issues of damnation and salvation in the way that *Lycidas* does. It does not introduce and then overcome "th' abhorrèd shears" but accepts the fatal stroke as terminal, constituting a limit and a frame within which imagery of natural process and epic figures can be used to define a human career. There is a maximum exploitation of what might be called horizontal reference; the figure and the career are attached to other human figures and careers, and to human careers in their heroic and symbolic embodiment in epic. In the epic context human actions have been shaped and formulated into a poetic action, a traditional epitome of the whole human voyage; the merest allusion to such a context may import both traditional dignity or stature and some of the poetic, dramatic, and symbolic concentration. So the Nisus and Euryalus allusion imports both rivalry and friendship, rivalry in the traditional metaphor of a race, and friendship as a dramatized ideal, together with a more general suggestion of the universal struggle of achievement, fraught with ardors and misfortunes yet withal a game and a formality and a ceremony, a celebration of those who have gone before and a ritual continuation. The whole poem, by adopting a traditional form, avails itself of ritual formulae, both extending and muting praise and pathos in the conventionalized figure of the victor and in the venerable *hail and farewell*. A. E. Housman's *To an Athlete Dying Young* offers a modern instance of this technique, employing the traditional metaphors of the athlete and the race and the ritual pose of the laurel-crowned victor.

The remarkable compression of Dryden's Marcellus allusion that does justice to will and to fate, to victory and defeat at once, accomplishes also the distancing of the human figure among the shades where he becomes composite, general, and whence the vision of his victorious stance is reported only by the privilege of poetry. Such a poem presents man by way of permanent symbols of nature and established symbols of art; it is a concentrated statement of the human condition with the recognition of limits and the celebration of achievement perfectly wrought together. The statement is complete, the symmetry unflawed. Within the accepted frame the poetic achievement is effective and powerful.

One way of seeing the distance that lies between *To Mr. Oldham* and *To Anne Killigrew* is to move directly from the encompassing fate of the former to fate as it appears in the last stanza of the latter:

> When in the Valley of *Jehosaphat,*
> The Judging God shall close the Book of Fate.

(ll. 180-81; I, 465K)

The classical vocabulary is here contained within the Christian vocabulary; the saint's legend, Christ's atonement, and Christian eschatology lie beyond tragedy and epic. The power of fate is still acknowledged in classical terms:

> Not Wit, nor Piety could Fate prevent;
> Nor was the cruel *Destiny* content
> To finish all the Murder at a Blow,
> To sweep at once her Life, and Beauty too.

(ll. 153-56; I, 464K)

And even beyond the acknowledgment of fate there lies one term of the classical vocabulary, apotheosis; this term is present in the translation of the dead to a position among the stars, a continuing, propitious influence upon the world below. In the final scene, however, the horizon is lifted, not for a mere *deus ex machina* but for the very God, and not for God contained in a classical name, not an *all-judging Jove* but *the Judging God* and in the valley of Jehosaphat.

The poem does have a way of speaking the classical and Christian languages together, but not directly with respect to Deity. Dryden's way of aligning the classical and Christian traditions was a skillful defensive accomplishment, particularly under the conditions of his age. On the one hand, the persistent suggestion of an *ethical* congruity between classical models and Christian ideals put the classical tradition in a position most likely to embarrass the assaults of a narrow Puritanical righteousness. On the other hand, the consistent affiliation of Christian ideals with an urbane, literate, cultured, humane tradition was calculated to defend the Christian tradition from the reductive, obscurantist phase of Puritan attack that would grind down the developed system of thought and forms of worship to a meager remainder of inspiration, zeal, and fervor. Dryden's way of associating the two traditions blunts the charge of paganism leveled against the classical tradition and fortifies the Christian tradition against a mean vulgarization.

Dryden's poetic strategy does not allow Christian thunder to become the sole prerogative of the Puritans. In *To Anne Killigrew,*

165

Christian imagery of the fall acknowledges and denounces the vices of the stage and the sins of the age. This attack anticipates by twelve years Jeremy Collier's cruder thunderings against the stage, and is the more effective for having the *mea culpa* attitude of the publican. The moral energy of Dryden's attack does not issue in a shrill or bawling righteous fervor, but deepens into a recognition of personal involvement in a general sinfulness. There is refinement as well as energy in this denunciation; a circle of grace is drawn about the Puritan polarity of sin and righteousness. Puritan zeal led to restriction, suppression, prohibition, but Dryden channels fervor into a prayer for atonement and regeneration. By taking this traditional Christian direction, the poem opens the way for consideration of the right use of what has been abused and can proceed to define the regeneration as aesthetic as well as moral, and classical as well as Christian. Poetry has sinned and a poet acknowledges the sin; the way is opened for the appropriate atonement for poetry, an atoning poet.

The generalizing of Anne Killigrew has both an aesthetic and a moral direction, with the classical vocabulary supported by the Christian in the account of aesthetic achievement, and the Christian vocabulary supported by the classical in the account of moral achievement. The sacred poet is the limit attained in the former case, and the atoning saint is the limit attained in the latter case. The collocation is possibly not so bold as, say, an allegorization of Christ as Hercules, where theology and mythology strikingly mingle, and yet there is here an accommodation of sacred and secular and of Christian and classical tradition that is only less striking, perhaps, because it is more gradually produced, with few surface prominences, and is managed in a whole series of tiny allegorizations that are suggested rather than pronounced, quiet accommodations and gestures of accommodation. Such, for example, are the smooth affiliation of vestal virgin and nun, and the gliding transition from an Arethusian chasteness and poetic purity to a sinless, atoning purity; such is the judgment of Anne Killigrew's character by the stoic austerity of Epictetus, where a classical ethical standard is moved toward an atoning figure, and, conversely, the saintly figure toward a classical ideal so that there is a slight dislocation of both; such is the blending of the nativity of a poetess with hints of the nativity of the Savior, and the suggested divine event with the music of the spheres. The complex affiliation of classical and Christian in the aesthetic and moral careers is such that the close articulation resists the narrow entering wedge of Puritanism. The poem, moreover, is not a bare two-part harmony but a rich interweaving of classical and Christian elements, supporting and amplifying each other in a manifold harmony. The paradise at the beginning and the last judgment at the end are filled with music. The frame begins in music, and it is music that untunes the sky.

There is a reflection of the range of Dryden's poetry in the range of his methods of using imagery. A performance like *Absalom and Achitophel,* where history bulks large, exhibits one phase of the achievement of his organizing and generalizing power. Imagery here begins in the analogy of two histories and rises from that double base to a value analogy. The other phase appears in a performance like *To Anne Killigrew,* where generalization is not grappling with a host of particulars, but proceeding easily, with the help of convention, from the narrow personal base to imagery that suggests analogies between two systems of value. One phase of his achievement finds the city brick and leaves it marble. In the other phase of his achievement, his imagery makes a monument in marble with a classical and a Christian face. This whole achievement gives richness, in Dryden's final decade, to the range and maturity of his reflectiveness; the poem addressed to the Duchess of Ormond becomes a poem about poetry and *To Mr. Congreve* a wry smile and an ironically finished reflection on the career of a poet, the life of the artist.

NOTES

1. *The Diary of John Evelyn,* ed. E. S. de Beer (6 vols., Oxford, 1955) III, 246, 259, 262.

2. See Pope's lines in the third of his *Moral Essays:*
Where London's column, pointing at the skies,
Like a tall bully, lifts the head, and lyes.
(Epistle III, To Bathurst, ll. 339-40)

3. *The Elizabethan World Picture* (New York: Macmillan Co., 1944), p. 94.

4. See above, p. 119, where Professor Bush's statement is quoted.

5. *Lives of the Poets,* ed. G. B. Hill (3 vols., Oxford, 1905), I, 164-65.

6. See *Paradise Lost,* IX, ll. 670-75 and X, ll. 306-08.

7. *A Discourse concerning the Original and Progress of Satire,* II, 612K.

Index

Absalom's Conspiracy, 90n.
Achitophel, or the Picture of a Wicked Politician, 90n
Ad conservandum animi pacem, 108
Addison, Joseph, 21
Aeneid, 14, 16, 93, 95, 143
Anatomy of the World, An (The First Anniversary), 5, 52, 123-24, 129n
Aristotle, 13, 158
Arius, 64-65
Arnold, Matthew, ix, 22
Ars Poetica (Horace), 72
Athanasius, Bishop of Alexandria, 64, 163
Auden, W. H., 3
Augustus, Emperor, 13, 96, 102

BATHURST, Ralph (1620-1704), Vice-Chancellor of Oxford, 40
Behn, Mrs. Aphra, 2
Biathanatos, 71
Boethius, 36
Boileau, Nicholas, 158
Bradshaw, John, 36
Breda, Declaration of, 12
Brome, Richard, 3
Brutus, Marcus Junius, 39
Busby, Dr. Richard, 3
Bush, Douglas, 119, 155
Butler, James. *See* Ormond, second Duke of

CAESAR, Julius, 39, 160
Camus, Albert, 131
Carpenter, Nathanael, 90n
Cato (the elder), 160
Charles I, 18, 28, 48-49, 76, 90n, 153, 157

Charles II, 1, 10, 11, 13-16, 35, 42, 49, 73, 76, 80, 84, 87-89, 149, 150, 162
Chaucer, Geoffrey, 17, 36, 119, 120, 139, 140, 141, 142, 143, 146
Cicero, 99, 158
Clarendon, Earl of (Edward Hyde), 2, 12
Cleopatra, 130
Cleveland, John, 4
Collier, Jeremy, 166
Congreve, William, 1, 133-38
Cook, John, regicide, 149
Cooper, Anthony Ashley. *See* Shaftesbury, Earl of
Cotton, Charles, 4
Cowley, Abraham, 4
Cranach, Lucas, 91n
Critical History of the Old Testament, The, 55
Cromwell, Oliver, 7, 8, 10, 35, 36, 76

DAVENANT, Sir William, 7
David, King of Israel, 14, 73-89, 151, 162
Davies, Sir John, 119
Defence of Poesy, The (Sidney's), 121
Defense of the English People, 157
Denham, Sir John, 3, 6
De Rerum Natura, 43
Diary of John Evelyn, The, 35, 49, 149-50
Diogenes, 108
Donne, John, 4, 5, 6, 14, 18, 22, 30, 52, 118, 123-25, 129n, 148, 151, 153, 155
Dorset, Earl of (Charles Sackville), 139
Driden, John, 139

169

Drury, Elizabeth, 52, 123-26, 153
Dryden, John, works of: *Absalom and Achitophel*, x, 13, 72-91, 92, 150, 155, 161, 162, 167; pref. to, 73, 74, 81, 154. *Aeneis* (tr.), 95, 96, 131; ded. of, 22, 159. *Annus Mirabilis*, 2, 7, 18, 150; ded. of, 150. *Astraea Redux*, ix, 1, 10, 13, 18, 19. *Eleonora*, ix, 123; pref. to, 98. Epilogues to—*Albion and Albanius*, 29; *All For Love*, 32, 34; *Amboyna*, 160; *The Man of Mode*, 32; *Opening the New House*, 33; *Oxford, 1674*, 40, 160; *The Princess of Cleves*, 26; *The Unhappy Favourite*, 50. *Fables, The*, 138; pref. to, 139. *Heroique Stanzas to . . . Cromwell*, 1, 7-9, 18. *Hind and the Panther, The*, 130. *Lines to Honor Dryden*, 8. *Mac Flecknoe*, 153. *Pollio*, Virgil's Fourth Eclogue (tr.), 147n. Prologues to—*Albion and Albanius*, 26, 37; *Albumazar*, 28; *All For Love*, 45-46, 147n; *Amboyna*, 26, 37; *Aureng-Zebe*, 49; *Circe*, 33; *Conquest of Granada*, I, 24, 31; *Conquest of Granada*, II, 34; *Duke of Guise*, 37, 48, 50; *H. R. H. Return from Scotland*, 37; *Kind Keeper*, 28; *Love Triumphant*, 132; *Loyal Brother*, 26, 28, 38; *Loyal General*, 25, 28, 50, 152; *Oedipus*, 24, 160; *Opening the New House*, 47, 160; *Oxford, 1673*, 39, 43, 51, 159; *Oxford, 1674*, 28, 40, 51, 160; *Oxford, 1676*, 41, 51, 160; *Oxford, 1680*, 51; *Oxford, 1681*, 42, 51; *Secret Love*, 26, 160; *Spanish Fryar*, 35; *The Tempest*, 26, 47, 50; *To King and Queen*, 38; *Unhappy Favourite*, 29, 50; *Witt without Money*, 28. *Religio Laici*, x, xi, 55-71, 72, 93, 158, 162, 163; pref. to, 49. *Secular Masque, The*, 132. *Song for St. Cecilia's Day, 1687, A*, 154. *To . . . Anne Killigrew*, xi, 98-129, 160, 161, 163, 164, 165-67. *To Her Grace The Dutchess of Ormond*, 90n, 139-47. *To His Sacred Majesty, A Panegyrick on His Coronation*, 1. *To John Hoddesdon, On His Divine Epigrams*, 1, 8. *To Mr. Congreve*, 132, 133-38, 167. *To the Memory of Mr. Oldham*, xi, 92-98, 163-64. *To My Honored Friend, Dr. Charleton*, 2. *To My Honored Friend, Sir Robert Howard*, 1. *To my Honour'd Kinsman*, 133. *To My Lord Chancellor*, 2. *To the Lady Castlemaine, upon Her Incouraging His First Play*, 2. *Upon the Death of the Lord Hastings*, 1, 3-8, 9, 18. *Wild Gallant, The*, 20

Dunciad, The, 138, 153

Edward, II, 136
Edward III, 136
Eikon Basilike, 18, 48
Eliot, T. S., x, 98
Encheiridion, 108
Epictetus, 108-9, 123, 128n, 129n, 166
Epistle III (To Bathurst), 167n
Essay on Man, An, 62, 63, 71n
Etherege, Sir George, 135
Evelyn, John, 35, 49, 149-50
Exodus, Book of, 40, 91n
Ezekiel, Book of, 127-28

Faerie Queene, The, 17, 128n
First Anniversary, The (An Anatomy of the World), 5, 52, 123-24, 129n
Fletcher, John, 20, 26, 135
Funeral Elegy, A, 124

Gaunt, John of, 88
Genesis, Book of, 59
Georgics (Virgil's), 102
Gondibert, 7
Gray, Thomas, 4
Gwyn, Ellen, 2

Hamlet, Prince of Denmark, 46, 88
Hastings, Lord Henry, 3
Henry IV, 155
Herrick, Robert, 3
Hesiod, 14
Hobbes, Thomas, 38, 47, 148
Holy Sonnet VII, 118, 129n
Homer, 140, 141, 142, 146, 159
Horace (Quintus Horatius Flaccus), 56, 72
Housman, A. E., 164
Hyde, Edward. *See* Clarendon, Earl of

Ignorant Book-Collector, The, 128n
In Memory of W. B. Yeats, 3
Ireton, Henry, 36
Isaiah, Book of, 16, 91n, 128n
Isocrates, Grecian orator, 99

James II, 49
Job, Book of, 91n
Joel, Book of, 91n, 127
John, Gospel of, 59, 128n
Johnson, Samuel, ix, 2, 4, 11, 20, 56, 58, 61, 80, 86, 87, 88, 89, 90, 118, 156
Jones, Col. John, regicide, 149
Jonson, Ben, 21, 26, 52, 123
Juvenal, 97, 140

Keats, John, 98
Killigrew, Anne, daughter of Henry Killigrew, 98-129, 166
King, Edward, 3
Kinsley, James, 75, 76, 108
Knight's Tale, The, 17, 36, 141, 142, 146

Landor, Walter Savage, 56
Legouis, Pierre, 108, 128n
Leviathan, 47
Lives (Plutarch's *Parallel Lives of the Most Eminent Greeks and Romans*), 73
Locke, John, 148
Lucian (of Samosata), 108, 128n
Lucretius, 42, 43
Luke, Gospel of, 150
Lycidas, 121, 129n, 156, 163, 164

Mack, Maynard, 129n
Marcellus, Marcus Claudius, nephew of Augustus, 95, 96, 97, 164
Marcellus, Marcus Claudius, Roman general, 95, 96, 97, 164
Marvell, Andrew, 3, 49
Mason, William, 4
Matthew, Gospel of, 86
Metamorphoses, 14
Milton, John, 3, 17, 77, 78, 79, 106-7, 116, 118, 119, 120, 121, 127, 129n, 131, 140, 147, 155, 157-59
Mittner, Matthias, 108
Monk, Samuel H., 129n
Monmouth, Duke of (James Scott), 84, 89
Montague, Charles, 139
Mutability Cantos, 36

Naboth's Vineyard, 90n
Needham, Marchamont, 4
Nero, Emperor, 157, 160
New Testament, 85, 86, 142, 151

Nokes, James, 31
Noyes, George R., 75, 76, 108

Oldham, John, 93-98
Old Testament, 85, 142, 151
On the Morning of Christ's Nativity, 106, 116, 120
Orchestra, 102
Origen, 74, 108
Ormond, Duchess of (Lady Mary Somerset), 139, 140, 142, 144, 167
Ormond, second Duke of (James Butler), 142, 143, 144
Ovid, 14, 139

Paradise Lost, 17, 77, 78, 79, 88, 121, 122, 156-58
Paradise Regained, 82, 83, 85
Pelagius, 65
Pilgrim, The, 20
Pindar, 99
Plantagenet, 142
Plato, 79, 104, 105, 106, 141, 143, 158
Pliny (the younger), 99
Plutarch, 73, 158
Pollio, Virgil's Fourth Eclogue, 16, 142, 144
Pope, Alexander, 22, 62, 63, 138, 153, 167n
Progress of the Soul, Of the (The Second Anniversary), 123-24
Psalms, Book of, 91n
Punic War, the Second, 96
Pythagoras, 106

Rainbow, Dr., 150
Raphael, 135
Reason of Church Government, The, 121
Reliquiae Sacrae Carolinae. Or the Works of that Great Monarch and Glorious Martyr King Charles I, 48
Richard II, 88
Rymer, Thomas (Tom the Second), 136, 138

Sackville, Charles. *See* Dorset, Earl of
Samuel, Second Book of, 73, 79, 85
Santayana, George, 132
Sappho, 104, 107, 112, 123
Scipio, Publius Cornelius (Africanus), 135
Scot, Major, regicide, 149

171

Scott, James. *See* Monmouth, Duke of
Scott, Sir Walter, ix, 4, 6, 75, 76, 118, 138
Scrope, Col. Adrian, regicide, 149
Second Anniversary, The (Of the Progress of the Soul), 123-24
Second Defense of the English People, 157
Seneca, 158
Shadwell, Thomas (Tom the First), 70, 136, 138
Shaftesbury, Earl of (Anthony Ashley Cooper), 76, 79
Shakespeare, William, 21, 25, 26, 36, 37, 47, 88, 137, 155
Shelley, Percy Bysshe, 3
Sidney, Sir Philip, 121
Simon, Richard (Father Simon), 56
Smith, D. Nichol, 69
Socrates, 64, 160, 163
Somerset, Lady Mary. *See* Ormond, Duchess of
Sophocles, 160
Southerne, Thomas, 135
Spenser, Edmund, 17, 19, 36, 128n
Sternhold, Thomas, 70, 71

Steward, Mrs. Elizabeth, 139
Suetonius, 91n
Syracuse, city in Sicily, 96

Theogeny (Hesiod's), 14
Thomson, James, 111, 112
Tillyard, E. M. W., 102, 105, 107, 109-12, 119-20, 154
Titus, Emperor, 91n
To an Athlete Dying Young, 164
Tonson, Jacob, 131

VANBRUGH, Sir John, 20
Van Doren, Mark, ix, 1, 4, 8-9, 138
Verrall, A. W., 56, 76-77, 89
Virgil, 14, 16, 17, 95, 96, 97, 102, 140, 141, 142, 143, 144, 146, 159
Vitruvius, 134

WALLERSTEIN, Ruth, 3, 4, 6
Westminster School, 3
William III, 131
Wren, Sir Christopher, 134
Wycherley, William, 135

YEATS, William Butler, 142